Contents

Breads, Scones & Teabreads

Biscuits, Cookies, Brownies, Traybakes & Buns

The Baking Cookbook

Practical recipes with step-by-step instructions

STAR
FIRE

Publisher and Creative Director: Nick Wells
Art Director: Mike Spender
Project Editor: Cat Emslie
Editorial Planning: Toria Lyle
Layout Design: Lucy Robins,
and Mike Spender and Colin Rudderham (original edition)
Digital Design and Production: Chris Herbert and Claire Walker

08 10 12 11 09

1 3 5 7 9 10 8 6 4 2

This edition first published in 2008 by
STAR FIRE
Crabtree Hall, Crabtree Lane,
Fulham, London, SW6 6TY
United Kingdom

www.star-fire.co.uk

STAR FIRE is part of The Foundry Creative Media Company Limited

© 2008 this edition The Foundry Creative Media Co. Ltd

ISBN 978-1-84786-191-7

The CIP record for this book is available from the British Library.

Printed in China

Authors: Catherine Atkinson, Juliet Barker, Gina Steer, Vicki Smallwood,
Carol Tennant, Mari Mererid Williams, Elizabeth Wolf-Cohen and Simone Wright
Editorial (original edition): Sara Goulding and Sara Robson
Photography: Colin Bowling, Paul Forrester and Stephen Brayne
Home Economists and Stylists: Jacqueline Bellefontaine,
Mandy Phipps, Vicki Smallwood and Penny Stephens

All props supplied by Barbara Stewart at Surfaces

NOTE
Recipes using uncooked eggs should be avoided by infants,
the elderly, pregnant women and anyone suffering from an illness.

Baked Puddings

Hygiene in the Kitchen

It is important to remember that many foods can carry some form of bacteria. In most cases, the worst it will lead to is a bout of food poisoning or gastroenteritis, although for certain people this can be serious. The risk can be reduced or eliminated, however, by good hygiene and proper cooking.

Do not buy food that is past its sell-by date and do not consume food that is past its use-by date. When buying food, use the eyes and nose. If the food looks tired, limp or a bad colour or it has a rank, acrid or simply bad smell, do not buy or eat it under any circumstances.

Take special care when preparing raw meat and fish. A separate chopping board should be used for each, and the knife, board and your hands should be thoroughly washed before handling or preparing any other food.

Regularly clean, defrost and clear out the refrigerator or freezer – it is worth checking the packaging to see exactly how long each product is safe to freeze. Avoid handling food if suffering from an upset stomach as bacteria can be passed on through food preparation.

Dish cloths and tea towels must be washed and changed regularly. Ideally use disposable cloths which should be replaced on a daily basis. More durable cloths should be left to soak in bleach, then washed in the washing machine at a high temperature.

Keep your hands, cooking utensils

and food preparation surfaces clean and do not allow pets to climb on to any work surfaces.

Buying

Avoid bulk buying where possible, especially fresh produce such as meat, poultry, fish, fruit and vegetables. Fresh foods lose their nutritional value rapidly, so buying a little at a time minimises loss of nutrients. It also means your fridge won't be so full, which reduces the effectiveness of the refrigeration process.

When buying prepackaged goods such as cans or pots of cream and yogurts, check that the packaging is intact and not damaged or pierced at all. Cans should not be dented, pierced or rusty. Check the sell-by dates even for cans and packets of dry ingredients such as flour and rice. Store fresh foods in the refrigerator as soon as possible – not in the car or the office.

When buying frozen foods, ensure that they are not heavily iced on the outside and that the contents feel completely frozen. Ensure that the frozen foods have been stored in the cabinet at the correct storage level and the temperature is below -18°C/ -0.4°F. Pack in cool bags to transport home and place in the freezer as soon as possible after purchase.

Preparation

Make sure that all work surfaces and utensils are clean and dry. Hygiene should be given priority at all times. Separate chopping boards should be used for raw and cooked meats, fish and vegetables. Currently, a variety of good quality plastic boards come in various designs and colours. This makes differentiating easier and the plastic has the added hygienic advantage of being washable at high temperatures in the dishwasher.

If using the board for fish, first wash in cold water, then in hot to prevent odour. Also remember that knives and utensils should always be thoroughly cleaned after use.

When cooking, be particularly careful to keep cooked and raw food separate to avoid any contamination. It is worth washing all fruits and vegetables regardless of whether they are going to be eaten raw or lightly cooked.

This rule should apply even to prewashed herbs and salads.

Do not reheat food more than once. If using a microwave, always check that the food is piping hot all the way through – in theory, the food should reach 70°C/158°F and needs to be cooked at that temperature for at least three minutes to ensure that all bacteria are killed.

All poultry must be thoroughly thawed before using, including chicken and poussin. Remove the food to be thawed from the freezer and place in a shallow dish to contain the juices. Leave the food in the refrigerator until it is completely thawed. A 1.4 kg/ 3 lb whole chicken will take about 26–30 hours to thaw. To speed up the process, immerse the chicken in cold water, making sure that the water is changed regularly. When the joints can move freely and no ice crystals remain in the cavity, the bird is completely thawed.

Once thawed, remove the wrapper and pat the chicken dry. Place the chicken in a shallow dish, cover lightly and store as close to the base of the refrigerator as possible. The chicken should be cooked as soon as possible.

Some foods can be cooked from frozen including many prepacked foods such as soups, sauces, casseroles and breads. Where applicable follow the manufacturers' instructions.

Vegetables and fruits can also be cooked from frozen, but meats and fish should be thawed first. The only time food can be refrozen is when the food has been thoroughly thawed then cooked. Once the food has cooled then it can be frozen again, but it should only be stored for one month.

All poultry and game (except for duck) must be cooked thoroughly. When cooked, the juices will run clear on the thickest part of the bird – the best area to try is usually the thigh. Other meats, like minced meat and pork should be cooked right the way through. Fish should turn opaque, be firm in texture and break easily into large flakes.

When cooking leftovers, make sure they are reheated until piping hot and that any sauce or soup reaches boiling point first.

Storing, Refrigerating and Freezing

Meat, poultry, fish, seafood and dairy products should all be refrigerated. The temperature of the refrigerator should be between 1–5°C/34–41°F while the freezer temperature should not rise above -18°C/-0.4°F.

To ensure the optimum refrigerator and freezer temperature, avoid leaving the door open for long periods of time.

Try not to overstock the refrigerator as this reduces the airflow inside and therefore the effectiveness in cooling the food within.

When refrigerating cooked food, allow it to cool down quickly and completely before refrigerating. Hot food will raise the temperature of the refrigerator and possibly affect or spoil other food stored in it.

Food within the refrigerator and freezer should always be covered. Raw and cooked food should be stored in separate parts of the refrigerator. Cooked food should be kept on the top shelves of the refrigerator, while raw meat, poultry and fish should be placed on bottom shelves to avoid drips and cross-contamination. It is recommended that eggs should be refrigerated in order to maintain their freshness and shelf life.

Take care that frozen foods are not stored in the freezer for too long. Blanched vegetables can be stored for one month; beef, lamb, poultry and pork for six months and unblanched vegetables and fruits in syrup for a year. Oily fish and sausages should be stored for three months. Dairy products can last four to six months, while cakes and pastries should be kept in the freezer for three to six months.

High Risk Foods

Certain foods may carry risks to people who are considered vulnerable such as the elderly, the ill, pregnant women, babies, young infants and those suffering from a recurring illness.

It is advisable to avoid those foods listed below which belong to a higher-risk category.

There is a slight chance that some eggs carry the bacteria salmonella. Cook the eggs until both the yolk and the white are firm to eliminate this risk. Pay particular attention to dishes and products incorporating lightly cooked or raw eggs which should be eliminated from the diet. Hollandaise sauce, mayonnaise, mousses, soufflés and meringues all use raw or lightly

cooked eggs, as do custard-based dishes, ice creams and sorbets. These are all considered high-risk foods to the vulnerable groups mentioned above.

Certain meats and poultry also carry the potential risk of salmonella and so should be cooked thoroughly until the juices run clear and there is no pinkness left. Unpasteurised products such as milk, cheese (especially soft cheese), pâté, meat (both raw and cooked) all have the potential risk of listeria and should be avoided.

When buying seafood, buy from a reputable source which has a high turnover to ensure freshness. Fish should have bright clear eyes, shiny skin and bright pink or red gills. The fish should feel stiff to the touch, with a slight smell of sea air and iodine. The flesh of fish steaks and fillets should be translucent with no signs of discolouration. Molluscs such as scallops, clams and mussels are sold fresh and are still alive. Avoid any that are open or do not close when tapped lightly. In the same way, univalves such as cockles or winkles should withdraw back into their shells when lightly prodded. When choosing cephalopods such as squid and octopus they should have a firm flesh and pleasant sea smell.

As with all fish, whether it is shellfish or seafish, care is required when freezing it. It is imperative to check whether the fish has been frozen before. If it has been frozen, then it should not be frozen again under any circumstances.

Essential Ingredients

The quantities may differ, but basic baking ingredients do not vary greatly. Let us take a closer look at the baking ingredients that are essential.

Fat

Butter and firm block margarine are the fats most commonly used in baking. Others can also be used such as white vegetable fat, lard and oil.

Low-fat spreads are not recommended for baking as they break down when cooked at a high temperature. Often it is a matter of personal preference which fat you choose when baking but there are a few guidelines that are important to remember.

Unsalted butter is the fat most commonly used in cake making, especially in rich fruit cakes and the heavier sponge cakes such as Madeira or chocolate torte. Unsalted butter gives a distinctive flavour to the cake. Some people favour margarine which imparts little or no flavour to the cake. As a rule, firm margarine and butter should not be used straight from the refrigerator but allowed to come to room temperature before using. Also, it should be beaten by itself first before creaming or rubbing in. Soft margarine is best suited to one-stage recipes. If oil is used care should be taken – it is a good idea to follow a specific recipe as the proportions of oil to flour and eggs are different.

Fat is an integral ingredient when making pastry, and again there are a few specific guidelines to bear in mind.

For shortcrust pastry the best results are achieved by using equal amounts of lard or white vegetable fat with butter or block margarine. The amount of fat used is always half the amount of flour. Other pastries use differing amounts of ingredients. Pâté sucrée (a sweet flan pastry) uses all butter with eggs and a little sugar, while flaky or puff pastry uses a larger proportion of fat to flour and relies on the folding and rolling during making to ensure that the pastry rises and flakes well. When using a recipe, refer to the instructions to obtain the best result.

Flour

A wide range of flour is available, all designed for specific jobs. Strong flour which is rich in gluten, whether it is white or brown (this includes granary and stoneground) is best kept for bread and Yorkshire pudding. It is also recommended for steamed suet puddings as well as puff pastry. oo flour is designed for pasta making and there is no substitute for this flour. Ordinary flour or weak flour is best for cakes, biscuits and sauces – they absorb fats easily and give a soft, light texture. This flour comes in plain white or self-raising, as well as wholemeal varieties. Self-raising flour, which has the raising agent already incorporated, is best kept for sponge cakes where it is important that an even rise is achieved. Plain flour can be used for all types of baking and sauces. If using plain flour for scones or cakes and puddings, unless otherwise stated in the recipe, use

1 teaspoon of baking powder to 225 g/ 8 oz of plain flour. With sponge cakes and light fruit cakes, it is best to use self-raising flour as the raising agent has already been added to the flour. This way there is no danger of using too much, which can result in a sunken cake with a sour taste. There are other raising agents that are also used. Some cakes use bicarbonate of soda with or without cream of tartar, blended with warm or sour milk. Whisked eggs also act as a raising agent as the air trapped in the egg ensures that the mixture rises. Generally no other raising agent is required.

Flour also comes ready sifted. There is even a special sponge flour designed especially for whisked sponges. It is also possible to buy flours that cater for coeliacs which contain no gluten. Buckwheat, soya and chick pea flours are also available.

Eggs

When a recipe states 1 egg, it is generally accepted this refers to a medium egg. Over the past few years the grading of eggs has changed. For years, eggs were sold as small, standard and large, then this method changed and they were graded in numbers with 1 being the largest. The general feeling by the public was that this system was misleading, so now we buy our eggs as small, medium and large. Due to the slight risk of salmonella, all eggs are now sold date stamped to ensure that the eggs are used in their prime. This applies even to farm eggs which are no longer allowed to be sold straight from the farm. Look for the lion quality stamp (on 75% of all eggs sold) which guarantees that the eggs come from hens vaccinated against salmonella, have been laid in the UK and are produced to the highest food safety and standards. All of these eggs carry a best before date.

There are many types of eggs sold and it really is a question of personal preference which ones are chosen. All offer the same nutritional benefits. The majority of eggs sold in this country are caged eggs. These are the cheapest eggs and the hens have been fed on a manufactured mixed diet.

Barn eggs are from hens kept in barns who are free to roam within the barn. However, their diet is similar to caged hens and the barns may be overcrowded.

It is commonly thought that free-range eggs are from hens that lead a much more natural life and are fed natural foods. This, however, is not always the case and in some instances they may still live in a crowded environment.

Four-grain eggs are from hens that have been fed on grain and no preventative medicines have been included in their diet. Organic eggs are from hens that live in a flock, whose beaks are not clipped and who are completely free to roam. Obviously, these eggs are much more expensive than the others.

Store eggs in the refrigerator with the round end uppermost (as packed in the egg boxes). Allow to come to room temperature before using. Do remember, raw or semi-cooked eggs should not be given to babies, toddlers, pregnant women, the elderly and those suffering from a reccurring illness.

Sugar

Sugar not only offers taste to baking but also adds texture and volume to the mixture. It is generally accepted that caster sugar is best for sponge cakes, puddings and meringues. Its fine granules disperse evenly when creaming or whisking. Granulated sugar is used for more general cooking, such as stewing fruit, whereas demerara sugar with its toffee taste and crunchy texture is good for sticky puddings and cakes such as flapjacks. For rich fruit cakes, Christmas puddings and cakes, use the muscovado sugars, which give a rich intense molasses or treacle flavour. Icing sugar is used primarily for icings but can also be used in meringues and in fruit sauces when the sugar needs to dissolve quickly. You could also try flavouring your own sugar. Place a vanilla pod in a screw top jar, fill with caster sugar, screw down the lid and leave for 2–3 weeks before using. Top up after use or use thinly pared lemon or orange rind in the same manner.

If trying to reduce sugar intake then use the unrefined varieties, such as golden granulated, golden caster, unrefined demerara and the muscovado sugars. All of these are a little sweeter than their refined counterparts, so less is required. Alternatively, clear honey or fructose (fruit sugar) can reduce sugar intake as they have similar calories to sugar, but are twice as sweet. Also, they have a slow release so their effect lasts longer. Dried fruits can also be included in the diet to top up sugar intake.

Yeast

There is something very comforting about the aroma of freshly baked bread, and the taste is far different and superior to commercially made bread. Bread making is regarded by some as being a time consuming process, but with the advent of fast-acting yeast this no longer applies. There are three types of yeast available: fresh yeast, which can now be bought in the instore bakery department of many supermarkets (fresh yeast freezes well); dried yeast, which is available in tins; and quick-acting yeast which comes in packets.

Fresh yeast should be bought in small quantities; it has a putty-like colour and texture with a slight wine smell. It should be creamed with a little sugar and some warm liquid before being added to the flour. Dried yeast can be stored for up to six months and comes in small hard granules. It should be sprinkled on to warm liquid with a little sugar then left to stand, normally between 15–20 minutes, until the mixture froths. When replacing the fresh yeast with dried yeast, use 1 tablespoon of dried yeast for 25 g/1 oz of fresh yeast.

Quick acting yeast cuts down the time of bread making and eliminates the need for proving the bread twice. Also, the yeast can be added straight to the flour without it needing to be activated. When replacing quick-acting yeast for dried yeast, you will need double the amount.

When using yeast, the most important thing to remember is that yeast is a living plant and needs food, water and warmth to work.

Equipment

Nowadays, you can get lost in the cookware sections of some of the larger stores – they really are a cook's paradise with gadgets, cooking tools and state-of-the-art electronic devices. A few, well-picked, high quality utensils and pieces of equipment will be frequently used and will therefore be a much wiser buy than cheaper gadgets.

Cooking equipment not only assists in the kitchen, but can make all the difference between success and failure. Take the humble cake tin: although a very basic piece of cooking equipment, it plays an essential role in baking. Using the incorrect size can be a disaster, as a tin that is too large will spread the mixture too thinly and the result will be a flat, limp-looking cake. On the other hand, cramming the mixture into a tin which is too small will result in the mixture rising up and out of the tin.

Baking Equipment

To ensure successful baking it is worth investing in a selection of high quality tins, which if looked after properly should last for many years. Follow the manufacturer's instructions when first using and ensure that the tins are thoroughly washed and dried after use and before putting away. Perhaps the most useful of tins for

baking are sandwich cake tins, ideal for classics such as Victoria sponge, genoese and coffee and walnut cake. You will need two tins and they are normally 18 cm/7 inches or 20.5 cm/8 inches in diameter, about 5–7.5cm/2–3 inches deep, and are often non stick.

With deep cake tins, it is personal choice whether you buy round or square tins, and they vary in size from 12.5–35.5 cm/5–14 inches with a depth of between 12.5–15 cm/5–6 inches. A deep cake tin, for everyday fruit or Madeira cake is a must – a useful size is 20.5 cm/8 inches.

Loaf tins are used for bread, fruit or tea bread and terrines and normally come in two sizes, 450 g/1 lb and 900 g/2 lb.

Good baking sheets are a must for all cooks. Dishes that are too hot to handle such as apple pies should be placed directly on to a baking tray. Meringues, biscuits and cookies are also cooked on a baking tray. Do not confuse these with Swiss roll tins which have sides all around: a sheet only has one raised side.

Square or oblong shallow baking tins are also very useful for making tray bakes, fudge brownies, flapjacks and shortbread.

Patty tins are ideal for making small buns, jam tarts or mince pies, while

individual Yorkshire pudding tins and muffin tins or flan tins are also useful. They are available in a variety of sizes.

There are plenty of other tins to choose from, ranging from themed tins, such as Christmas tree shapes and numbers from 1–9, as well as tins shaped as petals, ring mould tins, (tins with a hole in the centre) and spring-form tins where the sides release after cooking allowing the finished cake to be removed easily.

Three to four different sizes of mixing bowls are also very useful.

Another piece of equipment which is worth having is a wire cooling rack. It is essential when baking to allow biscuits and cakes to cool after being removed from their tins.

A selection of different-sized roasting tins are also a worthwhile investment as they can double up as a bain marie, or for cooking larger quantities of cakes such as gingerbread. A few different tins and dishes are required if baking crumbles, soufflés and pies. Ramekin dishes and small pudding basins can be used for a variety of different recipes, as can small tartlet tins and dariole moulds. When purchasing your implements for baking, perhaps the rolling pin is one of the most important. Ideally it should be long and thin, heavy enough to roll the pastry out easily but not too heavy that it is uncomfortable to use. Pastry needs to be rolled out on a flat surface, and although a lightly floured flat surface will do, a marble slab will keep the pastry cool and ensure that the fats do not melt while being rolled. This helps to keep the pastry light, crisp and flaky rather than heavy and stodgy, which happens if the fat melts before being baked.

Other useful basic pastry implements are tools such as a pastry brush (which can be used to wet pastry or brush on a glaze), a pastry wheel for cutting and a sieve to remove impurities and also to sift air into the flour, encouraging the pastry or mixture to be lighter in texture.

Basic mixing cutlery is also essential, such as a wooden spoon (for mixing and creaming), a spatula (for transferring the mixture from the mixing bowl to the baking tins and spreading the mixture once it is in the tins) and a palette knife (to ease cakes

and breads out of their tins before placing them on the wire racks to cool). Measuring spoons and cups are essential for accurate measuring of both dry and wet ingredients.

Electrical Equipment

Nowadays help from time-saving gadgets and electrical equipment make baking far more easy and quick. Equipment can be used for creaming, mixing, beating, whisking, kneading, grating and chopping. There is a wide choice of machines available from the most basic to the very sophisticated.

Food Processors

When choosing a machine, you must first decide what you need your processor to do. If you are a novice to baking, it may be a waste to start with a machine that offers a wide range of implements and functions. This can be off-putting and result in not using the machine to its full capabilities.

In general, while styling and product design play a role in the price, the more you pay, the larger the machine will be, with a bigger bowl capacity and many more gadgets attached. Nowadays, you can chop, shred, slice, chip, blend, purée, knead, whisk and cream anything. However, just what basic features should you ensure your machine has before buying it?

When buying a food processor look for measurements on the side of the processor bowl and machines with a removable feed tube which allows food or liquid to be added while the motor is still running. Look out for machines that have the facility to increase the capacity of the bowl (ideal when making soup) and have a pulse button for controlled chopping.

For many, storage is also an issue, so reversible discs and flex storage, or on more advanced models, a blade storage compartment or box, can be advantageous.

It is also worth thinking about machines that offer optional extras that

can be bought as your cooking requirements change. For instance, mini chopping bowls are available for those wanting to chop small quantities of food. If time is an issue, dishwasher-friendly attachments may be vital. Citrus presses, liquidisers and whisks may all be useful attachments for the individual cook.

Blenders

Blenders often come as attachments to food processors and are generally used for liquidising and puréeing foods. There are two main types of blender. The first is known as a goblet blender. The blades of this blender are at the bottom of the goblet with measurements up the sides. The second blender is portable. It is hand-held and should be placed in a bowl to blend.

Food Mixers

These are ideally suited to mixing cakes and kneading dough, either as a table-top mixer or a hand-held mixer. Both are extremely useful and based on the same principle of mixing or whisking in an open bowl to allow more air to get to the mixture and therefore give a lighter texture.

The table-top mixers are freestanding and are capable of dealing with fairly large quantities of mixture. They are robust machines, capable of easily dealing with kneading dough and heavy cake mixing as well as whipping cream, whisking egg whites or making one-stage cakes. These mixers also offer a wide range of attachments ranging from liquidisers, mincers, juicers, can openers and many more and varied attachments.

Hand-held mixers are smaller than freestanding mixers and often come with their own bowl and stand from which they can be lifted off and used as hand-held devices. They have a motorised head with detachable twin whisks. These mixers are particularly versatile as they do not need a specific bowl in which to whisk. Any suitable mixing bowl can be used.

Basic Techniques

There is no mystery to successful baking, it really is easy providing you follow a few simple rules and guidelines. First, read the recipe right through before commencing. There is nothing more annoying than getting to the middle of a recipe and discovering that you are minus one or two of the ingredients. Until you are confident with a recipe do not try any short cuts, or you may find that you have left out a vital step which means that the recipe cannot work. Most of all, have patience, baking is easy – if you can read, you can bake.

Pastry Making

Pastry needs to be kept as cool as possible throughout. Cool hands help, but are not essential. Use cold or iced water, but not too much as pastry does not need to be wet. Make sure that your fat is not runny or melted but firm (this is why block fat is the best). Avoid using too much flour when rolling out as this alters the proportions, and also avoid handling the dough too much. Roll in one direction as this helps to ensure that the pastry does not shrink. Allow the pastry to rest after rolling, preferably in the refrigerator. If you follow these guidelines but still your pastry is not as good as you would like it to be, then make it in a processor instead.

Lining a Flan Case

It is important to choose the right tin to bake with. You will often find that a loose-bottomed metal flan case is the best option as it conducts heat more efficiently and evenly than a ceramic dish. It also has the added advantage of a removable base, which makes the transfer of the final flan or tart a much simpler process; it simply lifts out, keeping the pastry intact.

Roll the pastry out on a lightly floured surface ensuring that it is a few inches larger than the flan case. Wrap the pastry around the rolling pin, lift and place in the tin. Carefully ease the pastry into the base and sides of the tin, ensuring that there are no gaps or tears in the pastry. Allow to rest for a few minutes then trim the edge either with a sharp knife or by rolling a rolling pin across the top of the flan tin.

Baking Blind

The term baking blind means that the pastry case needs to be cooked without the filling, resulting in a crisp pastry shell that is either partially or fully cooked depending on whether the filling needs any cooking. Pastry shells can be prepared ahead of time, as they last for several days if stored correctly in an airtight container or longer if frozen.

To bake blind, line a pastry case with the prepared pastry and allow to rest in the refrigerator for 30 minutes. This will help to minimise shrinkage while it is being cooked. Remove from the refrigerator and lightly prick the base all over with a fork (do not do this if the filling is runny). Brush with a little beaten egg if desired or simply line the case with a large square of greaseproof paper, big enough to cover both the base and sides of the pastry case. Fill with either ceramic baking beans or dried beans. Place on a baking sheet and bake in a preheated oven, generally at 200°C/400°F/Gas Mark 6, remembering that ovens can take at least 15 minutes to reach this heat. Cook for 10–12 minutes, then remove from the oven and discard the paper and beans. Return to the oven and continue to cook for a further 5–10 minutes depending on whether the filling needs cooking. As a rule, unless otherwise stated, individual pastry tartlet cases also benefit from baking blind.

Covering a Pie Dish

To cover a pie, roll out the pastry until it is about two inches larger than the circumference of the dish. Cut a 2.5 cm/1 inch strip from around the outside of the pastry and then moisten the edge of the pie dish you are using. Place the strip on the edge of the dish

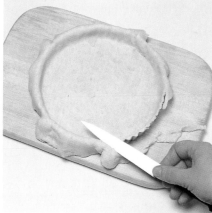
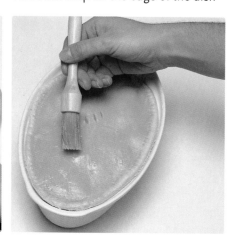

and brush with water or beaten egg. Generously fill the pie dish until the surface is slightly rounded. Using the rolling pin, lift the remaining pastry and cover the pie dish. Press together, then seal. Using a sharp knife, trim off any excess pastry from around the edges. Try to avoid brushing the edges of the pastry, especially puff pastry as this prevents the pastry rising evenly. Before placing in the oven make a small hole in the centre of the pie to allow the steam to escape.

The edges of the pie can be forked by pressing the back of a fork around the edge of the pie, or instead crimp by pinching the edge crust holding the thumb and index finger of your right hand against the edge while gently pushing with the index finger of your left hand. Other ways of finishing the pie are to knock up (achieved by gently pressing your index finger down on to the rim and, at the same time, tapping a knife horizontally along the edge giving it a flaky appearance), or fluting the edges by pressing your thumb down on the edge of the pastry while gently drawing back an all-purpose knife about 1 cm/½ inch and repeating around the rim. Experiment by putting leaves and berries made out of leftover pastry to finish off the pie, then brush the top of the pie with beaten egg.

Lining Cake Tins

If a recipe states that the tin needs lining, do not be tempted to ignore this. Rich fruit cakes and other cakes that take a long time to cook benefit from the tin being lined so that the edges and base do not burn or dry out. Greaseproof or baking parchment paper is ideal for this. It is a good idea to have the paper at least double thickness, or preferably 3–4 thicknesses. Sponge cakes and other cakes that are cooked in 30 minutes or less are also better if the bases are lined as it is far easier to remove them from the tin.

The best way to line a round or square tin is to lightly draw around the base and then cut just inside the markings so it sits easily inside the tin. Next, lightly oil the paper so it easily peels away from the cake. If the sides of the tin also need to be lined, then cut a strip of paper long enough for the tin. This can be measured by wrapping a piece of string around the rim of the tin. Once again, lightly oil the paper, push against the tin and oil once more as this will hold the paper to the sides of the tin. Steamed puddings usually need only a disc of greaseproof paper at the bottom of the dish as the sides come away easily.

Hints for Successful Baking

Ensure that the ingredients are accurately measured. A cake that has too much flour or insufficient egg will be dry and crumbly. Take care when measuring the raising agent if used, as too much will mean that the cake will rise too quickly and then sink. Insufficient raising agent means the cake will not rise in the first place.

Ensure that the oven is preheated to the correct temperature, remembering that it can take 10 minutes to reach 180°C/350°F/Gas Mark 4. You may find that an oven thermometer is a good investment. Cakes are best if cooked in the centre of the preheated oven. Do try to avoid the temptation of opening the oven door at the beginning of cooking as a draft can make the cake sink. If using a fan oven then refer to the manufacturer's instructions, as they normally cook 10–20° hotter than conventional ovens.

Check that the cake is thoroughly cooked by removing from the oven and inserting a clean skewer into the cake. Leave for 30 seconds and remove. If the skewer is completely clean then the cake is cooked; if there is a little mixture left on the skewer then return to the oven for a few minutes.

Other problems that you may encounter while cake making are insufficient creaming of the fat and sugar or a curdled creamed mixture (which will result in a densely textured and often fairly solid cake). Flour that has not been folded in carefully enough or has not been mixed with enough raising agent may also result in a fairly heavy consistency. It is very important to try to ensure that the correct size of tin is used as you may end up either with a flat, hard cake or one which has spilled over the edge of the tin. Another tip to be aware of (especially when cooking with fruit) is that if the consistency is too soft, the cake will not be able to support the fruit and it will sink to the bottom.

Finally, when you take your cake out of the oven, unless the recipe states that it should be left in the tin until cold, leave for a few minutes and then loosen the edges and turn out on to a wire rack to cool. Cakes that are left in the tin for too long, unless otherwise stated, tend to sink or slightly overcook.

When storing, make sure the cake is completely cold before placing it into an airtight tin or plastic container.

Culinary Terms Explained

Bain marie A French term, meaning water bath. A shallow tin, often a roasting tin, half-filled with water. Smaller dishes of food are then placed in it, allowing them to cook at lower temperatures without over-heating. This method is often used to cook custards and other egg dishes or to keep some dishes warm.

Baking blind The method often used for cooking the pastry case of flans and tarts before the filling is added. After lining the tin with the uncooked pastry it is then covered with a sheet of greaseproof or baking parchment paper and weighed down with either ceramic baking beans or dried beans and is baked in the oven as directed in the recipe.

Baking parchment paper Used for wrapping food to be cooked (*en papillote*) and for lining cake tins to prevent sticking.

Baking powder A raising agent that works by producing carbon dioxide as a consequence of a reaction caused by the acid and alkali ingredients that expand during the baking process. This causes breads and cakes to rise.

Beating The method by which air is introduced into a mixture using a fork, wooden spoon, whisk or electric mixer. Beating is also used as a method to soften ingredients.

Bicarbonate of soda This acts as a raising agent in baking when combined with liquid.

Binding Adding liquid or egg to bring a dry mixture together. Normally this entails using either a fork, spoon or your fingertips.

Blender An electric machine with rotating blades used mainly with soft and wet ingredients to purée and liquidise, although it can grind dry ingredients such as nuts and breadcrumbs.

Blending Dry ingredients are mixed with liquid to form a smooth paste before a boiling liquid is added. Used for thickening stews, casseroles, soups and sauces.

Brioche A traditional bread eaten in France for breakfast, usually served warm. Brioche has a rich, bread-like texture containing yeast and is baked in the shape of a small cottage loaf. A delicious substitute for bread in bread and butter pudding.

Caramel Obtained by heating sugar at a very low heat until it turns liquid and deep brown in colour. This is used in dishes such as crème caramel, which is baked in a bain marie.

Centigrade This is a scale for measuring the temperature within the oven (also known as celcius).

Choux A type of pastry (rather like a glossy batter) that is piped into small balls on to a baking tray and baked until light and airy. They can then be filled with cream or savoury fillings.

Cocotte Another name for a ramekin, a small, ovenproof earthenware pot used for individual portions.

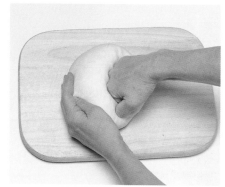

Cornstarch An American term for cornflour which is used to thicken consistency and can also be used in meringue-making to prevent the meringue becoming hard and brittle and to enhance its chewiness.

Cream of tartar Another raising agent often present in both self-raising flour and baking powder.

Creaming The method by which fat and sugar are beaten together until lighter in colour and fluffy. By creaming the fat in cake mixtures, air is incorporated into the fairly high fat content. It thus lightens the texture of cakes and puddings.

Crimping The fluted effect used for the decoration on pies or tarts created by pinching the edge crust while holding the thumb and index finger of your right hand against the edge and gently pushing with the index finger of your left hand.

Crumb The term by which flour and fat are combined typically for use in pastry, crumble and biscuits.

Curdle When the milk separates from a sauce through acidity or excessive heat. This can also happen to creamed cake mixtures that have separated due to the eggs being too cold or being added too quickly.

Dariole A small narrow mould with slopping sides used for making madeleines. Darioles can also be used for individual steamed or baked puddings and jellies.

Dough A dense mixture of flour, water and often yeast. Also used to describe raw pastry, scones and biscuit mixtures.

Dredging The sprinkling of food with a coating (generally of flour or sugar).

A board may be dredged with flour before the pastry is rolled out and cakes and biscuits can be dredged with sugar or icing sugar after baking.

Dropping consistency The consistency a cake or pudding mixture reaches before being cooked. It tends to be fairly soft (but not runny) and should drop off a spoon in around five seconds when tapped lightly on the side of a bowl.

Dust To sprinkle lightly, often with flour, sugar or icing sugar.

En croute Used to describe food which is covered with raw pastry and then baked.

En papillote A French term used to describe food which is baked, but is wrapped in greaseproof or baking parchment paper before cooking. This works well with fish as the aroma from the different herbs or spices and the fish are contained during cooking and not released until the paper parcel is opened.

Fermenting A term used during bread, beer or wine making to note the chemical change brought about through the use of a fermenting agent, such as yeast.

Filo A type of pastry that is wafer-thin. Three to four sheets are usually used at a time in baking.

Folding A method of combining creamed fat and sugar with flour in cake and pudding mixes usually by carefully mixing with a large metal spoon, either by cutting and folding, or by doing a figure of eight in order to maintain a light texture.

Glacé A French term meaning glossy or iced. Glacé icing is a quick icing often used to decorate cakes and biscuits. It is made using icing sugar and warm water.

Greaseproof paper Paper that tends to be relatively non-stick and which is used to line tins to prevent cakes and puddings from sticking.

Grinding Reducing hard ingredients such as nuts to crumbs, normally by the use of a grinder or a pestle and mortar

Knead The process of pummelling and working dough in order to strengthen the gluten in the flour and make the dough more elastic, thus giving a good rise. Also applies to pastry making; the dough is kneaded on a lightly floured surface to give a smooth and elastic pastry, making it easier to roll and ensuring an even texture after baking. In both cases the outside of the dough is drawn into the centre.

Knock back The term used for a second kneading after the dough has been allowed to rise. This is done to ensure an even texture and to disperse any large pockets of air.

Pasteurising The term given when milk and eggs are heated to destroy bacteria.

Piping The way in which cakes and desserts are decorated, or the method by which choux pastry is placed on to a baking sheet. This is achieved by putting cream, icing or mixture in a nylon bag (with a nozzle attached) and then slowly forcing the filling through the nozzle and piping it on to the cake or baking tray.

Proving The term used in breadmaking when the bread is allowed to rise a second time after it has been kneaded once and then shaped before it is baked.

Puff pastry Probably the richest of pastries. When making from the beginning, it requires the lightest of handling.

Ramekin An ovenproof, earthenware dish which provides an individual serving.

Rice paper This edible paper is made from the pith of a Chinese tree and can be used as a base on which to bake sticky cakes and biscuits such as almond macaroons.

Rubbing in The method of combining fat into flour for crumble toppings, shortcrust pastry, biscuits and scones.

Scalloping The term given to a type of pie decoration achieved by horizontal cuts made in the pastry which is then pulled back with the knife to produce a scalloped effect.

Sifting The shaking of dry ingredients (primarily flour) through a metal or nylon sieve to remove impurities and introduce air before using in baking.

Unleavened Often refers to bread that does not use a raising agent and is therefore flat, such as Indian naan bread.

Vol-au-vent Translated it means to fly or float on the wind. This small and usually round or oval puff pastry case is first baked and then filled with savoury meat, seafood or vegetable filling in a sauce.

Whipping/whisking The term given to incorporating air rapidly into a mixture (either through using a manual whisk or an electric whisk).

Zest Very thin, long pieces of the coloured part of an orange, lemon or lime peel, containing the fruit oil which is responsible for the citrus flavour. Normally a zester is used which removes the zest without any of the bitter white pith. (Rind refers to the peel which has been grated on a grater into very small pieces.)

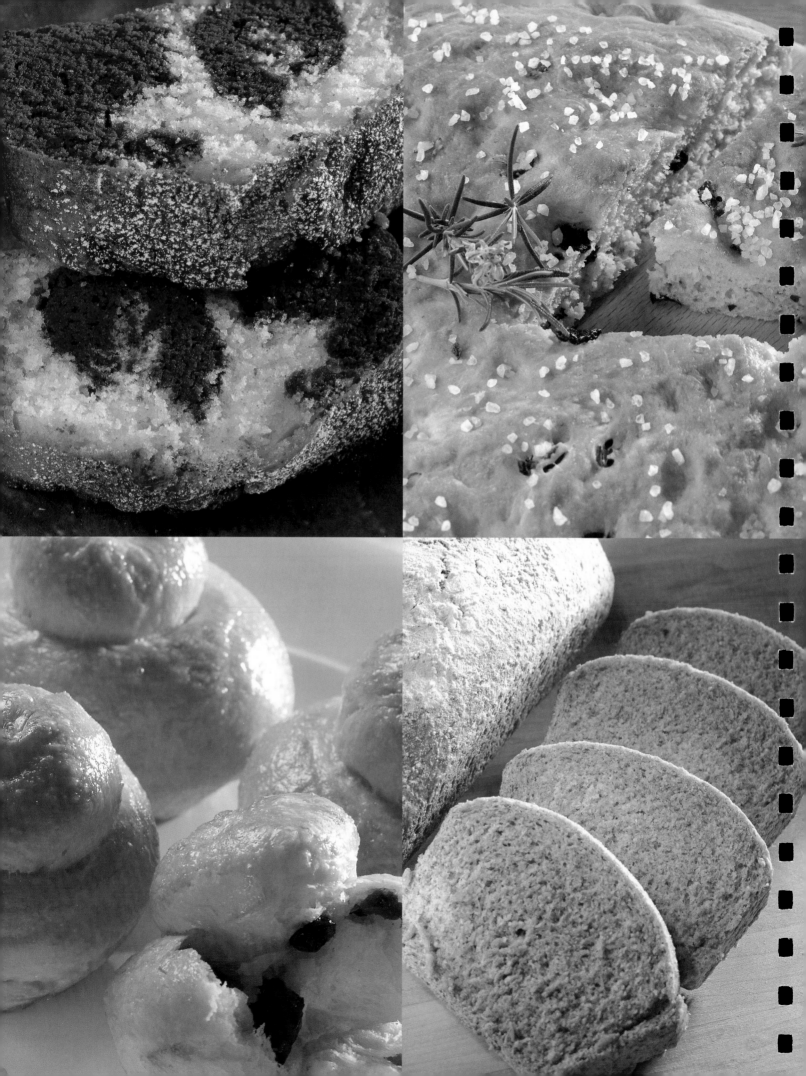

Breads, Scones & Teabreads

Where better to start baking than with this section which includes recipes for basics such as the Classic White Loaf? Follow easy step-by-step instructions to make delicious flavoured breads including Rosemary & Olive Focaccia and Spicy Filled Naan Bread. Or spoil yourself with something sweet like the tasty Marbled Chocolate & Orange Loaf.

Classic White Loaf

INGREDIENTS

Makes 1 x 900 g/2 lb loaf

700 g/1½ lb strong white flour
1 tbsp salt
25 g/1 oz butter, cubed
1 tsp caster sugar
2 tsp easy-blend dried yeast
150 ml/¼ pint milk
300 ml/½ pint warm water
1 tbsp plain flour, to dredge

Light wholemeal variation:

450 g/1 lb strong wholemeal flour
225 g/8 oz strong white flour
beaten egg, to glaze
1 tbsp kibbled wheat, to finish

TASTY TIP

Every now and then nothing can beat white bread, especially when it is freshly cooked. While the bread is still warm spread generously with fresh butter and eat. It is simply delicious!

1 Preheat the oven to 220°C/425°F/Gas Mark 7, 15 minutes before baking. Oil and line the base of a 900 g/2 lb loaf tin with greaseproof paper. Sift the flour and salt into a large bowl. Rub in the butter, then stir in the sugar and yeast. Make a well in the centre.

2 Add the milk and the warm water to the dry ingredients. Mix to a soft dough, adding a little more water if needed. Turn out the dough and knead on a lightly floured surface for 10 minutes, or until smooth and elastic.

3 Place the dough in an oiled bowl, cover with clingfilm or a clean tea towel and leave in a warm place to rise for 1 hour, or until doubled in size. Knead again for a minute or two to knock out the air.

4 Shape the dough into an oblong and place in the prepared tin. Cover with oiled clingfilm and leave to rise for a further 30 minutes or until the dough reaches the top of the tin. Dredge the top of the loaf with flour or brush with the egg glaze and scatter with kibbled wheat if making the wholemeal version. Bake the loaf on the middle shelf of the preheated oven for 15 minutes.

5 Turn down the oven to 200°C/400°F/Gas Mark 6. Bake the loaf for a further 20–25 minutes, or until well risen and hollow sounding when tapped underneath. Turn out, cool on a wire rack and serve.

1

2

4

Mixed Grain Bread

INGREDIENTS

Makes 1 large loaf

350 g/12 oz strong white flour

2 tsp salt

225 g/8 oz strong granary flour

125 g/4 oz rye flour

25 g/1 oz butter, diced

2 tsp easy-blend dried yeast

25 g/1 oz rolled oats

2 tbsp sunflower seeds

1 tbsp malt extract

450 ml/³/₄ pint warm water
  (see Helpful Hint)

1 medium egg, beaten

HELPFUL HINT

The amount of water you need to add to the dry ingredients in this recipe will depend on the type and brand of flour you use. Add just enough water to make a soft elastic dough.

1   Preheat the oven to 220°C/425°F/Gas Mark 7, 15 minutes before baking. Sift the white flour and salt into a large bowl. Stir in the Granary and rye flours, then rub in the butter until the mixture resembles breadcrumbs. Stir in the yeast, oats and seeds and make a well in the centre.

2   Stir the malt extract into the warm water until dissolved. Add the malt water to the dry ingredients. Mix to a soft dough.

3   Turn the dough out on to a lightly floured surface and knead for 10 minutes, until smooth and elastic.

4   Put in an oiled bowl, cover with clingfilm and leave to rise in a warm place for 1¹/₂ hours or until doubled in size.

5   Turn out and knead again for a minute or two to knock out the air.

6   Shape into an oval loaf about 30.5 cm/12 inches long and place on a well-oiled baking sheet.

7   Cover with oiled clingfilm and leave to rise for 40 minutes, or until doubled in size

8   Brush the loaf with beaten egg and bake in the preheated oven for 35–45 minutes, or until the bread is well risen, browned and sounds hollow when the base is tapped. Leave to cool on a wire rack, then serve.

2

4

8

Quick Brown Bread

INGREDIENTS

Makes 2 x 450 g/1 lb loaves

700 g/1½ lb strong wholemeal flour
2 tsp salt
½ tsp caster sugar
7 g/¼ oz sachet easy-blend
   dried yeast
450 ml/¾ pint warm water

To finish:
beaten egg, to glaze
1 tbsp plain white flour, to dust

Onion & caraway seed rolls:
1 small onion, peeled and
   finely chopped
1 tbsp olive oil
2 tbsp caraway seeds
milk, to glaze

HELPFUL HINT
For most breads the dough is kneaded, left to rise, kneaded, shaped and then left to rise again. This bread does not need the first rising – simply knead, shape, rise and bake.

1 Preheat the oven to 200°C/400°F/Gas Mark 6, 15 minutes before baking. Oil 2 x 450 g/1 lb loaf tins. Sift the flour, salt and sugar into a large bowl, adding the remaining bran in the sieve. Stir in the yeast, then make a well in the centre.

2 Pour the warm water into the dry ingredients and mix to form a soft dough, adding a little more water if needed.

3 Knead on a lightly floured surface for 10 minutes, until smooth and elastic.

4 Divide in half, shape into 2 oblongs and place in the tins. Cover with oiled clingfilm and leave in a warm place for 40 minutes, or until risen to the top of the tins.

5 Glaze 1 loaf with the beaten egg and dust the other loaf generously with the plain flour.

6 Bake the loaves in the preheated oven for 35 minutes or until well risen and lightly browned. Turn out of the tins and return to the oven for 5 minutes to crisp the sides. Cool on a wire rack.

7 For the onion and caraway seed rolls, gently fry the onion in the oil until soft. Reserve until the onions are cool, then stir into the dry ingredients with 1 tablespoon of the caraway seeds. Make the dough as before.

8 Divide the dough into 16 pieces and shape into rolls. Put on 2 oiled baking trays, cover with oiled clingfilm and prove for 30 minutes.

9 Glaze the rolls with milk and sprinkle with the rest of the seeds. Bake for 25–30 minutes, cool on a wire rack and serve.

1

4

5

Rustic Country Bread

INGREDIENTS

Makes 1 large loaf

Sourdough starter:
225 g/8 oz strong white flour
2 tsp easy-blend dried yeast
300 ml/½ pint warm water

Bread dough:
350 g/12 oz strong white flour
25 g/1 oz rye flour
1½ tsp salt
½ tsp caster sugar
1 tsp dried yeast
1 tsp sunflower oil
175 ml/6 fl oz warm water

To finish:
2 tsp plain flour
2 tsp rye flour

HELPFUL HINT
Put the remaining starter in a pan, stir in 125 ml/4 fl oz of warm water and 125 g/4 oz strong white flour. Stir twice a day for 2–3 days and use as a starter for another loaf.

1 Preheat the oven to 220°C/425°F/Gas Mark 7, 15 minutes before baking. For the starter, sift the flour into a bowl. Stir in the yeast and make a well in the centre. Pour in the warm water and mix with a fork.

2 Transfer to a saucepan, cover with a clean tea towel and leave for 2–3 days at room temperature. Stir the mixture and spray with a little water twice a day.

3 For the dough, mix the flours, salt, sugar and yeast in a bowl. Add 225 ml/8 fl oz of the starter, the oil and the warm water. Mix to a soft dough.

4 Knead on a lightly floured surface for 10 minutes until smooth and elastic. Put in an oiled bowl, cover and leave to rise in a warm place for about 1½ hours, or until doubled in size.

5 Turn the dough out and knead for a minute or two. Shape into a round loaf and place on an oiled baking sheet.

6 Cover with oiled clingfilm and leave to rise for 1 hour, or until doubled in size.

7 Dust the loaf with flour, then using a sharp knife make several slashes across the top of the loaf. Slash across the loaf in the opposite direction to make a square pattern.

8 Bake in the preheated oven for 40–45 minutes, or until golden brown and hollow sounding when tapped underneath. Cool on a wire rack and serve.

2

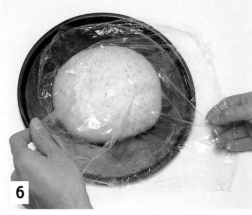

6

7

Soft Dinner Rolls

INGREDIENTS

Makes 16

50 g/2 oz butter

1 tbsp caster sugar

225 ml/8 fl oz milk

550 g/1¼ lb strong white flour

1½ tsp salt

2 tsp easy-blend dried yeast

2 medium eggs, beaten

To glaze and finish:

2 tbsp milk

1 tsp sea salt

2 tsp poppy seeds

HELPFUL HINT

For clover leaf rolls, divide into 3 equal pieces and roll each into a ball. Place the balls together in a triangular shape. For cottage buns, divide the dough into two-thirds and one-third pieces. Shape each piece into a round, then put the smaller one on top of the larger one. Push a floured wooden spoon handle or finger through the middle of the top one and into the bottom one to join together.

1 Preheat the oven to 220°C/425°F/Gas Mark 7, 15 minutes before baking. Gently heat the butter, sugar and milk in a saucepan until the butter has melted and the sugar has dissolved. Cool until tepid. Sift the flour and salt into a bowl, stir in the yeast and make a well in the centre. Reserve 1 tablespoon of the beaten eggs. Add the rest to the dry ingredients with the milk mixture. Mix to form a soft dough.

2 Knead the dough on a lightly floured surface for 10 minutes until smooth and elastic. Put in an oiled bowl, cover with clingfilm and leave in a warm place to rise for 1 hour, or until doubled in size. Knead again for a minute or two, then divide into 16 pieces. Shape into plaits, snails, clover leaf and cottage buns. For plaits, divide into 3 equal pieces and roll each piece of dough into a rope about 9 cm/3½ inches long. Plait, then pinch the ends together to seal. For snails, roll into a 25.5 cm/10 inch rope, then form into a coil, tucking the end under the roll to secure (also see Helpful Hints). Place on 2 oiled baking sheets, cover with oiled clingfilm and leave to rise for 30 minutes, until doubled in size.

3 Mix the reserved beaten egg with the milk and brush over the rolls. Sprinkle some with sea salt, others with poppy seeds and leave some plain. Bake in the preheated oven for about 20 minutes, or until golden and hollow sounding when tapped underneath. Transfer to a wire rack. Cover with a clean tea towel while cooling to keep the rolls soft and serve.

1

2

3

Bagels

INGREDIENTS

Makes 12

450 g/1 lb strong plain flour
1½ tsp salt
2 tsp easy-blend dried yeast
2 medium eggs
1 tsp clear honey
2 tbsp sunflower oil
250 ml/9 fl oz tepid water

To finish:

1 tbsp caster sugar
beaten egg, to glaze
2 tsp poppy seeds
½ small onion, peeled and
  finely chopped
2 tsp sunflower oil

TASTY TIP

Why not try bagels for breakfast? They are delicious filled with cheese and ham or served toasted with scrambled egg. They are also good with smoked salmon and cream cheese.

1   Preheat the oven to 200°C/400°F/Gas Mark 6, 15 minutes before baking. Sift the flour and salt into a large bowl. Stir in the yeast, then make a well in the centre. Whisk the eggs together with the honey and oil. Add to the dry ingredients with the tepid water and mix to form a soft dough.

2   Knead the dough on a lightly floured surface for 10 minutes until smooth and elastic. Put in a bowl, cover with clingfilm and leave in a warm place to rise for 45 minutes, or until doubled in size.

3   Briefly knead the dough again to knock out the air. Divide into 12 pieces, form each into a 20.5 cm/8 inch roll, curve into a ring and pinch the edges to seal.

4   Put the rings on an oiled baking sheet, cover with oiled clingfilm and leave to rise in a warm place for 20 minutes, or until risen and puffy.

5   Add the caster sugar to a large saucepan of water. Bring to the boil, then drop in the bagels, one at a time and poach for 15 seconds. Lift out with a slotted spoon and return to the baking tray.

6   Brush the bagels with beaten egg and sprinkle one-third with poppy seeds. Mix together the onion and oil and sprinkle over another third of the bagels. Leave the remaining third plain.

7   Bake in the preheated oven for 12–15 minutes, or until golden brown. Transfer to a wire rack and serve when cool.

1

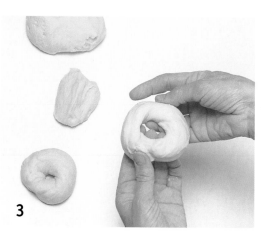

3

5

Breads, Scones & Teabreads

Sweet Potato Baps

INGREDIENTS

Makes 16

225 g/8 oz sweet potato
15 g/½ oz butter
freshly grated nutmeg
about 200 ml/7 fl oz milk
450 g/1 lb strong white flour
2 tsp salt
7 g/¼ oz sachet easy-blend yeast
1 medium egg, beaten

To finish:
beaten egg, to glaze
1 tbsp rolled oats

HELPFUL HINT

There are many varieties of sweet potato, so be sure to choose the correct potato for this recipe as their flavours and textures vary. The sweet potato used in this recipe is dark skinned and has a vibrant orange flesh which cooks to a moist texture.

1 Preheat the oven to 200°C/400°F/Gas Mark 6, 15 minutes before baking. Peel the sweet potato and cut into large chunks. Cook in a saucepan of boiling water for 12–15 minutes, or until tender.

2 Drain well and mash with the butter and nutmeg. Stir in the milk, then leave until barely warm.

3 Sift the flour and salt into a large bowl. Stir in the yeast. Make a well in the centre.

4 Add the mashed sweet potato and beaten egg and mix to a soft dough. Add a little more milk if needed, depending on the moisture in the sweet potato.

5 Turn out the dough on to a lightly floured surface and knead for about 10 minutes, or until smooth and elastic. Place in a lightly oiled bowl, cover with clingfilm and leave in a warm place to rise for about 1 hour, or until the dough doubles in size.

6 Turn out the dough and knead for a minute or two until smooth. Divide into 16 pieces, shape into rolls and place on a large oiled baking sheet. Cover with oiled clingfilm and leave to rise for 15 minutes.

7 Brush the rolls with beaten egg, then sprinkle half with rolled oats and leave the rest plain.

8 Bake in the preheated oven for 12–15 minutes, or until well risen, lightly browned and sound hollow when the bases are tapped. Transfer to a wire rack and immediately cover with a clean tea towel to keep the crusts soft.

4

6

8

Rosemary & Olive Focaccia

INGREDIENTS

Makes 2 loaves

700 g/1½ lb strong white flour
pinch of salt
pinch of caster sugar
7 g/¼ oz sachet easy-blend
   dried yeast
2 tsp freshly chopped rosemary
450 ml/¾ pint warm water
3 tbsp olive oil
75 g/3 oz pitted black olives, roughly
   chopped
sprigs of rosemary, to garnish

To finish:

3 tbsp olive oil
coarse sea salt
freshly ground black pepper

TASTY TIP

As a variation to the rosemary used in this bread, replace with chopped sun-dried tomatoes. Knead the tomatoes into the dough along with the olives in step 3, then before baking drizzle with the oil and replace the salt with some grated mozzarella cheese.

1 Preheat the oven to 200°C/400°F/Gas Mark 6, 15 minutes before baking. Sift the flour, salt and sugar into a large bowl. Stir in the yeast and rosemary. Make a well in the centre.

2 Pour in the warm water and the oil and mix to a soft dough. Turn out on to a lightly floured surface and knead for about 10 minutes, until smooth and elastic.

3 Pat the olives dry on kitchen paper, then gently knead into the dough. Put in an oiled bowl, cover with clingfilm and leave to rise in a warm place for 1½ hours, or until it has doubled in size.

4 Turn out the dough and knead again for a minute or two. Divide in half and roll out each piece to a 25.5 cm/10 inch circle.

5 Transfer to oiled baking sheets, cover with oiled clingfilm and leave to rise for 30 minutes.

6 Using the fingertips, make deep dimples all over the the dough. Drizzle with the oil and sprinkle with sea salt.

7 Bake in the preheated oven for 20–25 minutes, or until risen and golden. Cool on a wire rack and garnish with sprigs of rosemary. Grind over a little black pepper before serving.

3

4

6

Daktyla–style Bread

INGREDIENTS

Makes 1 loaf

350 g/12 oz strong white flour
125 g/4 oz wholemeal flour
1 tsp salt
50 g/2 oz fine cornmeal
2 tsp easy-blend dried yeast
2 tsp clear honey
1 tbsp olive oil
4 tbsp milk
250 ml/9 fl oz water

To glaze & finish:

4 tbsp milk
4 tbsp sesame seeds

FOOD FACT

Daktyla was traditionally made in Cyprus during Lent. The Cypriots made crisp syrup-soaked fingers of pastry filled with an almond and cinnamon filling. In this recipe the bread is shaped into oblongs and baked so that the bread can be broken into fingers to eat.

1 Preheat the oven to 220°C/425°F/Gas Mark 7, 15 minutes before baking. Sift the white and wholemeal flours and salt into a large bowl, adding the bran left in the sieve. Stir in the cornmeal and yeast. Make a well in the centre.

2 Put the honey, oil, milk and water in a saucepan and heat gently until tepid. Add to the dry ingredients and mix to a soft dough, adding a little more water if needed.

3 Knead the dough on a lightly floured surface for 10 minutes, until smooth and elastic. Put in an oiled bowl, cover with clingfilm and leave to rise in a warm place for 1½ hours or until it has doubled in size.

4 Turn the dough out and knead for a minute or two. Shape into a long oval about 25.5 cm/10 inches long. Cut the oval into 6 equal pieces. Shape each piece into an oblong, then on an oiled baking sheet arrange in a row so that all the pieces of dough are touching.

5 Cover with oiled clingfilm and leave for 45 minutes, or until doubled in size.

6 Brush the bread with milk, then scatter with sesame seeds.

7 Bake the bread in the preheated oven for 40–45 minutes, or until golden brown and hollow sounding when tapped underneath. Cool on a wire rack and serve.

2

4

6

Spicy Filled Naan Bread

INGREDIENTS

Makes 6

400 g/14 oz strong white flour
1 tsp salt
1 tsp easy-blend dried yeast
15 g/½ oz ghee or unsalted butter,
   melted
1 tsp clear honey
200 ml/7 fl oz warm water

For the filling:

25 g/1 oz ghee or unsalted butter
1 small onion, peeled and
   finely chopped
1 garlic clove, peeled and crushed
1 tsp ground coriander
1 tsp ground cumin
2 tsp grated fresh root ginger
pinch of chilli powder
pinch of ground cinnamon
salt and freshly ground
   black pepper

HELPFUL HINT

Ghee is more expensive than other butters but it has a longer life and a much higher smoke point (190°C/375°F). Ghee, therefore, is practical for sautèing and frying.

1 Preheat the oven to 220°C/450°F/Gas Mark 8, 15 minutes before baking and place a large baking sheet in to heat up. Sift the flour and salt into a large bowl. Stir in the yeast and make a well in the centre. Add the ghee or melted butter, honey and the warm water. Mix to a soft dough. dough.

2 Knead the dough on a lightly floured surface, until smooth and elastic. Put in a lightly oiled bowl, cover with clingfilm and leave to rise for 1 hour, or until doubled in size.

3 For the filling, melt the ghee or butter in a frying pan and gently cook the onion for about 5 minutes. Stir in the garlic and spices and season to taste with salt and pepper. Cook for a further 6–7 minutes, until soft. Remove from the heat, stir in 1 tablespoon of water and leave to cool.

4 Briefly knead the dough, then divide into 6 pieces. Roll out each piece of dough to 12.5 cm/5 inch rounds. Spoon the filling on to one half of each round.

5 Fold over and press the edges together to seal. Re-roll to shape into flat ovals, about 16 cm/6½ inches long.

6 Cover with oiled clingfilm and leave to rise for about 15 minutes.

7 Transfer the breads to the hot baking sheet and cook in the preheated oven for 10–12 minutes, until puffed up and lightly browned. Serve hot.

3

4

5

Fruited Brioche Buns

INGREDIENTS

Makes 12

225 g/8 oz strong white flour
pinch of salt
1 tbsp caster sugar
7 g/¼ oz sachet easy-blend
    dried yeast
2 large eggs, beaten
50 g/2 oz butter, melted
beaten egg, to glaze

For the filling:

40 g/1½ oz blanched
    almonds, chopped
50 g/2 oz luxury mixed
    dried fruit
1 tsp light soft brown sugar
2 tsp orange liqueur or brandy

1 Preheat the oven to 220°C/425°F/Gas Mark 7, 15 minutes before baking. Sift the flour and salt into a bowl. Stir in the sugar and yeast. Make a well in the centre. Add the eggs, butter and 2 tablespoons of warm water and mix to a soft dough.

2 Knead the dough on a lightly floured surface for 5 minutes, until smooth and elastic. Put in an oiled bowl, cover with clingfilm and leave to rise in a warm place for 1 hour, or until it has doubled in size.

3 Mix the ingredients for the filling together, cover the bowl and leave to soak while the dough is rising.

4 Re-knead the dough for a minute or two, then divide into 12 pieces. Take 1 piece at a time and flatten three-quarters into a 6.5 cm/2½ inch round. Spoon a little filling in the centre, then pinch the edges together to enclose. Put seam-side down into a well-greased fluted 12-hole bun tin.

5 Shape the smaller piece of dough into a round and place on top of the larger one.

6 Push a finger or floured wooden spoon handle through the middle of the top one and into the bottom one to join them together. Repeat with the remaining balls of dough.

7 Cover the brioche with oiled clingfilm and leave for about 20 minutes, or until well risen.

8 Brush the brioches with beaten egg and bake in the preheated oven for 10–12 minutes, or until golden. Cool on a wire rack and serve.

3

4

6

Spiced Apple Doughnuts

INGREDIENTS

Makes 8

225 g/8 oz strong white flour
¹/₂ tsp salt
1¹/₂ tsp ground cinnamon
1 tsp easy-blend dried yeast
75 ml/3 fl oz warm milk
25 g/1 oz butter, melted
1 medium egg, beaten
oil, to deep-fry
4 tbsp caster sugar, to coat

For the filling:

2 small eating apples, peeled, cored
 and chopped
2 tsp soft light brown sugar
2 tsp lemon juice

TASTY TIP

These doughnuts are also excellent when filled with pears. Simply replace the 2 apples with 2 pears and continue with the recipe. Look out for Comice pears as they are considered to be amongst the best on the market or use English Conference pears which have lovely tender melting flesh and a delicious flavour.

1 Sift the flour, salt and 1 teaspoon of the cinnamon into a large bowl. Stir in the yeast and make a well in the centre.

2 Add the milk, butter and egg and mix to a soft dough. Knead on a lightly floured surface for 10 minutes, until smooth and elastic.

3 Divide the dough into 8 pieces and shape each into a ball. Put on a floured baking sheet, cover with oiled clingfilm and leave in a warm place for 1 hour, or until doubled in size.

4 To make the filling, put the apples in a saucepan with the sugar, lemon juice and 3 tablespoons of water. Cover and simmer for about 10 minutes, then uncover and cook until fairly dry, stirring occasionally. Mash or blend in a food processor to a purée.

5 Pour enough oil into a deep-fat frying pan to come one-third of the way up the pan. Heat the oil to 180°C/350°F, then deep-fry the doughnuts for 1¹/₂–2 minutes on each side, until well browned.

6 Drain the doughnuts on kitchen paper, then roll in the caster sugar mixed with the remaining ¹/₂ teaspoon of ground cinnamon. Push a thick skewer into the centre to make a hole, then pipe in the apple filling. Serve warm or cold.

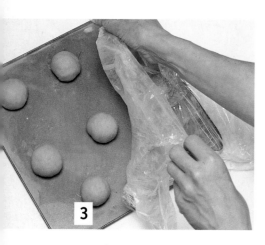

3

5

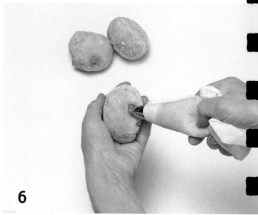

6

Bacon & Tomato Breakfast Twist

INGREDIENTS

Serves 8

450 g/1 lb strong plain flour
½ tsp salt
7 g/¼ oz sachet easy-blend
   dried yeast
300 ml/½ pint warm milk
15 g/½ oz butter, melted

For the filling:

225 g/8 oz back bacon, derinded
15 g/½ oz butter, melted
175 g/6 oz ripe tomatoes, peeled,
   deseeded and chopped
freshly ground black pepper

To finish:

beaten egg, to glaze
2 tsp medium oatmeal

1 Preheat the oven to 200°C/400°F/Gas Mark 6, 15 minutes before baking. Sift the flour and salt into a large bowl. Stir in the yeast and make a well in the centre. Pour in the milk and butter and mix to a soft dough.

2 Knead on a lightly floured surface for 10 minutes, until smooth and elastic. Put in an oiled bowl, cover with clingfilm and leave to rise in a warm place for 1 hour, until doubled in size.

3 Cook the bacon under a hot grill for 5–6 minutes, turning once until crisp. Leave to cool, then roughly chop.

4 Knead the dough again for a minute or two. Roll it out to a 25.5 x 33 cm/10 x 13 inch rectangle. Cut in half lengthways. Lightly brush with butter, then scatter with the bacon, tomatoes and black pepper, leaving a 1 cm/½ inch margin around the edges.

5 Brush the edges of the dough with beaten egg, then roll up each rectangle lengthways.

6 Place the 2 rolls side by side and twist together, pinching the ends to seal.

7 Transfer to an oiled baking sheet and loosely cover with oiled clingfilm. Leave to rise in a warm place for 30 minutes.

8 Brush with the beaten egg and sprinkle with the oatmeal. Bake in the preheated oven for about 30 minutes, or until golden brown and hollow sounding when tapped on the base. Serve the bread warm in thick slices.

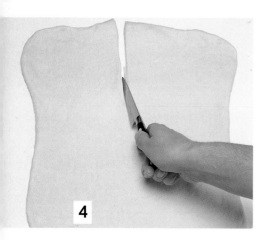
4

5

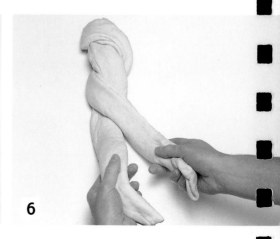
6

Irish Soda Bread

INGREDIENTS

Makes 1 loaf

400 g/14 oz plain white flour, plus 1
tbsp for dusting

1 tsp salt

2 tsp bicarbonate of soda

15 g/½ oz butter

50 g/2 oz coarse oatmeal

1 tsp clear honey

300 ml/½ pint buttermilk

2 tbsp milk

Wholemeal variation:

400 g/14 oz plain wholemeal flour,
plus 1 tbsp for dusting

1 tbsp milk

TASTY TIP

Soda bread relies on the raising agent bicarbonate of soda, which when combined with the acidic buttermilk enables the bread to rise. For an unusual Irish soda bread, knead a handful of currants and 2 tablespoons of caraway seeds in step 3. According to Irish legend the cross on the top of the bread is intended to scare away the devil.

1. Preheat the oven to 200°C/400°F/Gas Mark 6, 15 minutes before baking. Sift the flour, salt and bicarbonate of soda into a large bowl. Rub in the butter until the mixture resembles fine breadcrumbs. Stir in the oatmeal and make a well in the centre.

2. Mix the honey, buttermilk and milk together and add to the dry ingredients. Mix to a soft dough.

3. Knead the dough on a lightly floured surface for 2–3 minutes, until the dough is smooth. Shape into a 20.5 cm/8 inch round and place on an oiled baking sheet.

4. Thickly dust the top of the bread with flour. Using a sharp knife, cut a deep cross on top, going about halfway through the loaf.

5. Bake in the preheated oven on the middle shelf of the oven for 30–35 minutes or until the bread is slightly risen, golden and sounds hollow when tapped underneath. Cool on a wire rack. Eat on the day of making.

6. For a wholemeal soda bread, use all the wholemeal flour instead of the white flour and add an extra tablespoon of milk when mixing together. Dust the top with wholemeal flour and bake.

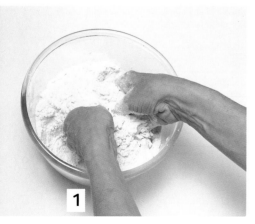

1

3

4

Traditional Oven Scones

INGREDIENTS

Makes 8

225 g/8 oz self-raising flour
1 tsp baking powder
pinch of salt
40 g/1½ oz butter, cubed
15 g/½ oz caster sugar
150 ml/¼ pint milk, plus
  1 tbsp for brushing
1 tbsp plain flour, to dust

Lemon & sultana scone variation:

50 g/2 oz sultanas
finely grated rind of ½ lemon
beaten egg, to glaze

TASTY TIP

Nothing beats scones still warm from the oven. Split the scones open and fill with a layer of juicy strawberry jam and clotted cream. Serve the scones with a pot of Earl Grey tea for a delicious afternoon treat.

1 Preheat the oven to 220°C/425°F/Gas Mark 7, 15 minutes before baking. Sift the flour, baking powder and salt into a large bowl. Rub in the butter until the mixture resembles fine breadcrumbs. Stir in the sugar and mix in enough milk to give a fairly soft dough.

2 Knead the dough on a lightly floured surface for a few seconds until smooth. Roll out until 2 cm/¾ inches thick and stamp out 6.5 cm/ 2½ inch rounds with a floured plain cutter.

3 Place on an oiled baking sheet and brush the tops with milk (do not brush it over the sides or the scones will not rise properly). Dust with a little plain flour.

4 Bake in the preheated oven for 12–15 minutes, or until well risen and golden brown. Transfer to a wire rack and serve warm or leave to cool completely. (The scones are best eaten on the day of baking but may be kept in an airtight tin for up to 2 days.)

5 For lemon and sultana scones, stir in the sultanas and lemon rind with the sugar. Roll out until 2 cm/¾ inches thick and cut into 8 fingers, 10 x 2.5 cm/4 x 1 inch in size. Bake the scones as before.

1

2

3

Cheese-crusted Potato Scones

INGREDIENTS

Makes 6

200 g/7 oz self-raising flour
25 g/1 oz wholemeal flour
½ tsp salt
1½ tsp baking powder
25 g/1 oz butter, cubed
5 tbsp milk
175 g/6 oz cold mashed potato
freshly ground black pepper

To finish:

2 tbsp milk
40 g/1½ oz mature Cheddar cheese,
   finely grated
paprika pepper, to dust
sprig of basil, to garnish

FOOD FACT

The scone supposedly acquired its name from the Stone of Destiny (or Scone) in Scotland where Scottish Kings were once crowned.

1   Preheat the oven to 220°C/425°F/Gas Mark 7, 15 minutes before baking. Sift the flours, salt and baking powder into a large bowl. Rub in the butter until the mixture resembles fine breadcrumbs.

2   Stir 4 tablespoons of the milk into the mashed potato and season with black pepper.

3   Add the dry ingredients to the potato mixture, mixing together with a fork and adding the remaining 1 tablespoon of milk if needed.

4   Knead the dough on a lightly floured surface for a few seconds until smooth. Roll out to a 15 cm/6 inch round and transfer to an oiled baking sheet.

5   Mark the scone round into 6 wedges, cutting about halfway through with a small sharp knife.

6   Brush with milk, then sprinkle with the cheese and a faint dusting of paprika.

7   Bake on the middle shelf of the preheated oven for 15 minutes, or until well risen and golden brown.

8   Transfer to a wire rack and leave to cool for 5 minutes before breaking into wedges.

9   Serve warm or leave to cool completely. Once cool store the scones in an airtight tin. Garnish with a sprig of basil and serve split and buttered.

1

5

6

Pecan & Lemon Loaf

INGREDIENTS

Cuts into 12 slices

350 g/12 oz plain flour
1 tsp baking powder
175 g/6 oz butter, cubed
75 g/3 oz caster sugar
125 g/4 oz pecan nuts, roughly
   chopped
3 medium eggs
1 tbsp milk
finely grated rind of 1 lemon
5 tbsp maple syrup

For the icing:

75 g/3 oz icing sugar
1 tbsp lemon juice
25 g/1 oz pecans,
   roughly chopped

FOOD FACT

Maple syrup is made using the sap of the maple tree and has an intensely sweet, almost vanilla flavour. It is important to differentiate between the real thing and cheaper imitations which are maple-flavoured syrups, and contain artificial flavours.

1 Preheat the oven to 170°C/325°F/Gas Mark 3, 10 minutes before baking. Lightly oil and line the base of a 900 g/2 lb loaf tin with non-stick baking parchment.

2 Sift the flour and baking powder into a large bowl.

3 Rub in the butter until the mixture resembles fine breadcrumbs. Stir in the caster sugar and pecan nuts.

4 Beat the eggs together with the milk and lemon rind. Stir in the maple syrup. Add to the dry ingredients and gently stir in until mixed thoroughly to make a soft dropping consistency.

5 Spoon the mixture into the prepared tin and level the top with the back of a spoon. Bake on the middle shelf of the preheated oven for 50–60 minutes, or until the cake is well risen and lightly browned. If a skewer inserted into the centre comes out clean, then the cake is ready.

6 Leave the cake in the tin for about 10 minutes, then turn out and leave to cool on a wire rack. Carefully remove the lining paper.

7 Sift the icing sugar into a small bowl and stir in the lemon juice to make a smooth icing.

8 Drizzle the icing over the top of the loaf, then scatter with the chopped pecans. Leave to set, thickly slice and serve.

4

5

8

Moist Mincemeat Tea Loaf

INGREDIENTS

Cuts into 12 slices

225 g/8 oz self-raising flour
½ tsp ground mixed spice
125 g/4 oz cold butter, cubed
75 g/3 oz flaked almonds
25 g/1 oz glacé cherries, rinsed, dried
  and quartered
75 g/3 oz light muscovado sugar
2 medium eggs
250 g/9 oz prepared mincemeat
1 tsp lemon zest
2 tsp brandy or milk

FOOD FACT

Traditionally mincemeat contained cooked lean beef, but this is now omitted. Mince pies are now part of the Christmas fare in Britain. There are many different recipes mostly containing suet. Again traditionally beef suet was used. With the upsurge in vegetarianism, however, vegetarian suet is now often used.

1   Preheat the oven to 180°C/350°F/Gas Mark 4, 10 minutes before cooking. Oil and line the base of a 900 g/2 lb loaf tin with non-stick baking paper.

2   Sift the flour and mixed spice into a large bowl. Add the butter and rub in until the mixture resembles breadcrumbs.

3   Reserve 2 tablespoons of the flaked almonds and stir in the rest with the glacé cherries and sugar.

4   Make a well in the centre of the dry ingredients. Lightly whisk the eggs, then stir in the mincemeat, lemon zest and brandy or milk.

5   Add the egg mixture and fold together until blended. Spoon into the prepared loaf tin, smooth the top with the back of a spoon, then sprinkle over the reserved flaked almonds.

6   Bake on the middle shelf of the preheated oven for 30 minutes. Cover with tinfoil to prevent the almonds browning too much. Bake for a further 30 minutes, or until well risen and a skewer inserted into the centre comes out clean.

7   Leave the tea loaf in the tin for 10 minutes before removing and cooling on a wire rack. Remove the lining paper, slice thickly and serve.

4

5

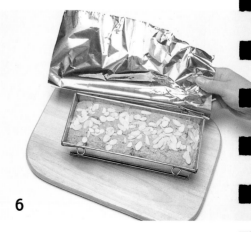
6

Marbled Chocolate & Orange Loaf

INGREDIENTS

Cuts into 6 slices

50 g/2 oz plain dark chocolate,
  broken into squares
125 g/4 oz butter, softened
125 g/4 oz caster sugar
zest of 1 orange
2 medium eggs, beaten
125 g/4 oz self-raising flour
2 tsp orange juice
1 tbsp cocoa powder, sifted

To finish:
1 tbsp icing sugar
1 tsp cocoa powder

TASTY TIP

To make a cream cheese icing for this cake, beat together 75 g/3 oz of cream cheese with 1–2 tablespoons of milk until smooth. Add a pinch of salt, 1 teaspoon of vanilla essence and 225 g/8 oz of icing sugar and mix well. Spread on top of the cake when cool.

1   Preheat the oven to 180°C/350°F/Gas Mark 4. Lightly oil a 450 g/1 lb loaf tin and line the base with a layer of non-stick baking paper.

2   Put the chocolate in a bowl over a saucepan of very hot water. Stir occasionally until melted. Remove and leave until just cool, but not starting to reset.

3   Meanwhile, cream together the butter, sugar and orange zest until pale and fluffy. Gradually add the beaten eggs, beating well after each addition.

4   Sift in the flour, add the orange juice and fold with a metal spoon or rubber spatula. Divide the mixture by half into 2 separate bowls. Gently fold the cocoa powder and chocolate into one half of the mixture.

5   Drop tablespoonfuls of each cake mixture into the prepared tin, alternating between the orange and chocolate mixtures. Briefly swirl the colours together with a knife to give a marbled effect.

6   Bake in the preheated oven for 40 minutes, or until firm and a fine skewer inserted into the centre comes out clean. Leave in the tin for 5 minutes, then turn out and cool on a wire rack. Carefully remove the lining paper.

7   Dust the cake with the icing sugar and then with the cocoa powder. Cut into thick slices and serve.

3

4

5

Fruity Apple Tea Bread

INGREDIENTS

Cuts into 12 slices

125 g/4 oz butter
125 g/4 oz soft light brown sugar
275 g/10 oz sultanas
150 ml/¼ pint apple juice
1 eating apple, peeled cored
  and chopped
2 medium eggs, beaten
275 g/10 oz plain flour
½ tsp ground cinnamon
½ tsp ground ginger
2 tsp bicarbonate of soda
curls of butter, to serve

To decorate:
1 eating apple, cored and sliced
1 tsp lemon juice
1 tbsp golden syrup, warmed

TASTY TIP

For an alcoholic version of this cake, soak the sultanas in brandy overnight before adding in step 2. To make the tea bread moister in texture, add 1 grated carrot at the same time as the chopped apple in step 3.

1. Preheat the oven to 180°C/350°F/Gas Mark 4. Oil and line the base of a 900 g/2 lb loaf tin with non-stick baking paper.

2. Put the butter, sugar, sultanas and apple juice in a small saucepan. Heat gently, stirring occasionally until the butter has melted. Tip into a bowl and leave to cool.

3. Stir in the chopped apple and beaten eggs. Sift the flour, spices and bicarbonate of soda over the apple mixture.

4. Stir into the sultana mixture, spoon into the prepared loaf tin and smooth the top level with the back of a spoon.

5. Toss the apple slices in lemon juice and arrange on top.

6. Bake in the preheated oven for 50 minutes. Cover with tinfoil to prevent the top from browning too much.

7. Bake for 30–35 minutes, or until a skewer inserted into the centre comes out clean.

8. Leave in the tin for 10 minutes before turning out to cool on to a wire rack.

9. Brush the top with golden syrup and leave to cool. Remove the lining paper, cut into thick slices and serve with curls of butter.

2

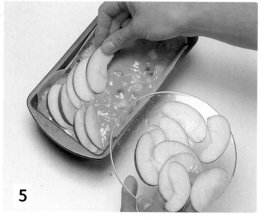

5

9

Biscuits, Cookies, Brownies, Traybakes & Buns

This section includes recipes for everyone's favourite treats that are so easy anyone can make them. Whether you fancy the simple Gingerbread or Fruit & Nut Flapjacks, or the more indulgent Triple Chocolate Brownies or Pecan Caramel Millionaire's Shortbread, this section will show you how to bake them.

Chocolate Chip Cookies

INGREDIENTS

Makes about 30

140 g/4½ oz butter
50 g/2 oz caster sugar
60 g/2½ oz soft dark brown sugar
1 medium egg, beaten
½ tsp vanilla essence
125 g/4 oz plain flour
½ tsp bicarbonate of soda
150 g/5 oz plain or milk chocolate chips

HELPFUL HINT

For light-textured, crumbly biscuits, do not over work the biscuit dough. Handle as little as possible and fold the ingredients together gently in a figure of 8 using a metal spoon or rubber spatula. To ring the changes with these basic biscuits, use an equal mixture of chocolate chips and nuts. Alternatively, replace the chocolate chips entirely with an equal quantity of your favourite chopped nuts.

1 Preheat the oven to 180°C/350°F/Gas Mark 4, 10 minutes before baking. Lightly butter 3–4 large baking sheets with 15 g/½ oz of the butter. Place the remaining butter and both sugars in a food processor and blend until smooth. Add the egg and vanilla essence and blend briefly. Alternatively, cream the butter and sugars together in a bowl, then beat in the egg with the vanilla essence.

2 If using a food processor, scrape out the mixture with a spatula and place the mixture into a large bowl. Sift the flour and bicarbonate of soda together, then fold into the creamed mixture. When the mixture is blended thoroughly, stir in the chocolate chips.

3 Drop heaped teaspoons of the mixture onto the prepared baking sheets, spaced well apart and bake the cookies in the preheated oven for 10–12 minutes or until lightly golden.

4 Leave to cool for a few seconds, then using a spatula, transfer to a wire rack and cool completely. The cookies are best eaten when just cooked, but can be stored in an airtight tin for a few days.

1

2

3

Fudgy Chocolate Bars

INGREDIENTS

Makes 14

25 g/1 oz glacé cherries
60 g/2½ oz shelled hazelnuts
150 g/5 oz plain dark chocolate
150 g/5 oz unsalted butter
½ tsp salt
150 g/5 oz digestive biscuits
1 tbsp icing sugar, sifted, optional

1 Preheat the oven to 180°C/350°F/Gas Mark 4, 10 minutes before baking. Lightly oil a 18 cm/7 inch square tin and line the base with nonstick baking parchment. Rinse the glacé cherries thoroughly, dry well on absorbent kitchen paper and reserve.

2 Place the nuts on a baking tray and roast in the preheated oven for 10 minutes, or until light golden brown. Leave to cool slightly, then chop roughly and reserve.

3 Break the chocolate into small pieces, place with the butter and salt into the top of a double boiler or in a bowl set over a saucepan of gently simmering water. Heat gently stirring until melted and smooth. Alternatively, melt the chocolate in the microwave, according to the manufacturer's instructions.

4 Chop the biscuits into 5 mm/¼ inch pieces and cut the cherries in half. Add to the chocolate mixture with the nuts and stir well. Spoon the mixture into the prepared tin and level the top.

5 Chill in the refrigerator for 30 minutes, remove from the tin, discard the baking parchment and cut into 14 bars. Cover lightly, return to the refrigerator and keep chilled until ready to serve. To serve, lightly sprinkle the bars with sifted icing sugar if using. Store covered in the refrigerator.

TASTY TIP

For these bars, it is best to use a plain chocolate with around 50 per cent cocoa solids. Dark chocolate would not give a good flavour as it is too bitter.

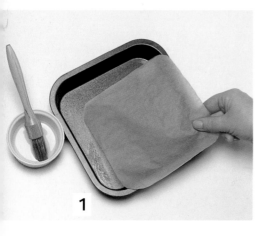

1

2

4

Italian Biscotti

INGREDIENTS

Makes 26–28

150 g/5 oz butter
200 g/7 oz caster sugar
¼ tsp vanilla essence
1 small egg, beaten
¼ tsp ground cinnamon
grated rind of 1 lemon
15 g/½ oz ground almonds
150 g/5 oz plain flour
150 g/5 oz plain dark chocolate

FOOD FACT

In Italy, these deliciously crunchy little biscuits are traditionally served with a sweet dessert wine called Vin Santo.

HELPFUL HINT

When using vanilla essence, do use essence, and not vanilla flavouring which is a cheap substitute. Alternatively, use vanilla caster sugar which is very easy to make. Simply place a vanilla pod in a clean screw top jar and fill with caster sugar. Secure and leave in a cool, dark place and leave for 2–3 weeks before using.

1 Preheat the oven to 190°C/375°F/Gas Mark 5, 10 minutes before baking. Lightly oil 3–4 baking sheets and reserve. Cream the butter and sugar together in a bowl and mix in the vanilla essence. When it is light and fluffy beat in the egg with the cinnamon, lemon rind and the ground almonds. Stir in the flour to make a firm dough.

2 Knead lightly until smooth and free from cracks. Shape the dough into rectangular blocks about 4 cm/1½ inches in diameter, wrap in greaseproof paper and chill in the refrigerator for at least 2 hours.

3 Cut the chilled dough into 5 mm/¼ inch slices, place on the baking sheets and cook in the preheated oven for 12–15 minutes or until firm. Remove from the oven, cool slightly, then transfer to wire racks to cool.

4 When completely cold, melt the chocolate in a heatproof bowl set over a saucepan of simmering water. Alternatively, melt the chocolate in the microwave according to the manufacturer's instructions. Spoon into a piping bag and pipe over the biscuits. Leave to dry on a sheet of nonstick baking parchment before serving.

1

2

4

Chocolate & Hazelnut Cookies

INGREDIENTS

Makes 12

75 g/3 oz blanched hazelnuts
100 g/3½ oz caster sugar
50 g/2 oz unsalted butter
pinch of salt
5 tsp cocoa powder
3 tbsp double cream
2 large egg whites
40 g/1½ oz plain flour
2 tbsp rum
75 g/3 oz white chocolate

HELPFUL HINT

Be careful not to chop the hazelnuts for too long in the food processor as this tends to make them very oily. To blanch hazelnuts (or any nut), simply place on a baking sheet and heat in a hot oven for 10 minutes. Remove, then place in a clean tea towel and rub off the brown skins. Do not rub too many at a time, otherwise they may escape from the tea towel.

1 Preheat the oven to 180°C/350°F/Gas Mark 4, 10 minutes before baking. Lightly oil and flour 2–3 baking sheets. Chop 25 g/1 oz of the hazelnuts and reserve. Blend the remaining hazelnuts with the caster sugar in a food processor until finely ground. Add the butter to the processor bowl and blend until pale and creamy.

2 Add the salt, cocoa powder and the double cream and mix well. Scrape the mixture into a bowl, using a spatula, and stir in the egg whites. Sift the flour, then stir into the mixture together with the rum.

3 Spoon heaped tablespoons of the batter onto the baking sheets and sprinkle over a few of the reserved hazelnuts. Bake in the preheated oven for 5–7 minutes or until firm. Remove the cookies from the oven and leave to cool for 1–2 minutes. Using a spatula, transfer to wire racks and leave to cool.

4 When the biscuits are cold, melt the chocolate in a heatproof bowl set over a saucepan of simmering water. Stir until smooth, then drizzle a little of the chocolate over the top of each biscuit. Leave to dry on a wire rack before serving.

1

2

3

Fig & Chocolate Bars

INGREDIENTS

Makes 12

125 g/4 oz butter
150 g/5 oz plain flour
50 g/2 oz soft light brown sugar
225 g/8 oz ready-to-eat dried figs,
  halved
juice of ½ a large lemon
1 tsp ground cinnamon
125 g/4 oz plain dark chocolate

1 Preheat the oven to 180°C/350°F/Gas Mark 4, 10 minutes before baking. Lightly oil a 18 cm/7 inch square cake tin. Place the butter and the flour in a large bowl and, using your fingertips, rub the butter into the flour until it resembles fine breadcrumbs.

2 Stir in the sugar, then using your hand, bring the mixture together to form a smooth dough. Knead until smooth then press the dough into the prepared tin. Lightly prick the base with a fork and bake in the preheated oven for 20–30 minutes or until golden. Remove from the oven and leave the shortbread to cool in the tin until completely cold.

3 Meanwhile, place the dried figs, lemon juice, 125 ml/4 fl oz water and the ground cinnamon in a saucepan and bring to the boil. Cover and simmer for 20 minutes or until soft, stirring occasionally during cooking. Cool slightly, then purée in a food processor until smooth. Cool, then spread over the cooked shortbread.

4 Melt the chocolate in a heatproof bowl set over a saucepan of simmering water. Alternatively, melt the chocolate in the microwave, according to the manufacturer's instructions. Stir until smooth, then spread over the top of the fig filling. Leave to become firm, then cut into 12 bars and serve.

HELPFUL HINT

If you are unable to find ready-to-eat figs, soak dried figs in boiling water for 20 minutes until plump. Drain well and use as above.

1

2

3

Chocolate-covered Flapjack

INGREDIENTS

Makes 24

215 g/7½ oz plain flour
150 g/5 oz rolled oats
225 g/8 oz light muscovado sugar
1 tsp bicarbonate of soda
pinch of salt
150 g/5 oz butter
2 tbsp golden syrup
250 g/9 oz plain dark chocolate
5 tbsp double cream

1 Preheat the oven to 180°C/350°F/Gas Mark 4, 10 minutes before baking. Lightly oil a 33 x 23 cm/13 x 9 inch Swiss roll tin and line with nonstick baking parchment. Place the flour, rolled oats, the light muscovado sugar, bicarbonate of soda and salt into a bowl and stir well together.

2 Melt the butter and golden syrup together in a heavy-based saucepan and stir until smooth, then add to the oat mixture and mix together thoroughly. Spoon the mixture into the prepared tin and press down firmly and level the top.

3 Bake in the preheated oven for 15–20 minutes or until golden. Remove from the oven and leave the flapjack to cool in the tin. Once cool, remove from the tin. Discard the parchment.

4 Melt the chocolate in a heatproof bowl set over a saucepan of gently simmering water. Alternatively, melt the chocolate in the microwave according to the manufacturer's instructions. Once the chocolate has melted quickly beat in the cream, then pour over the flapjack. Mark patterns over the chocolate with a fork when almost set.

5 Chill the flapjack in the refrigerator for at least 30 minutes before cutting into bars. When the chocolate has set, serve. Store in an airtight container for a few days.

HELPFUL HINT

Try lightly oiling your measuring spoon before dipping it into the golden syrup. The syrup will slide off the spoon easily. Alternatively, warm the syrup slightly before measuring.

2

4

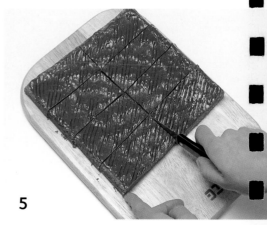

5

Shortbread Thumbs

INGREDIENTS

Makes 12

125 g/4 oz self-raising flour
125 g/4 oz butter, softened
25 g/1 oz white vegetable fat
50 g/2 oz granulated sugar
25 g/1 oz cornflour, sifted
5 tbsp cocoa powder, sifted
125 g/4 oz icing sugar
6 assorted coloured glacé cherries,
   rinsed, dried and halved

FOOD FACT

Using a combination of butter and vegetable fat gives these biscuits a softer texture than using all butter.

HELPFUL HINT

After baking, remove the cooked biscuits as soon as possible from the baking sheets as they will continue to cook and could overcook. Cool completely on wire cooling racks before storing in airtight tins.

1   Preheat the oven to 150°C/300°F/Gas Mark 2, 10 minutes before baking. Lightly oil 2 baking sheets. Sift the flour into a large bowl, cut 75 g/3 oz of the butter and the white vegetable fat into small cubes, add to the flour, then, using your fingertips, rub in until the mixture resembles fine breadcrumbs.

2   Stir in the granulated sugar, sifted cornflour and 4 tablespoons of cocoa powder and bring the mixture together with your hand to form a soft and pliable dough.

3   Place on a lightly floured surface and shape into 12 small balls. Place onto the baking sheets at least 5 cm/2 inches apart, then press each one with a clean thumb to make a dent.

4   Bake in the preheated oven for 20–25 minutes or until light golden brown. Remove from the oven and leave for 1–2 minutes to cool. Transfer to a wire rack and leave until cold.

5   Sift the icing sugar and the remaining cocoa powder into a bowl and add the remaining softened butter. Blend to form a smooth and spreadable icing with 1–2 tablespoons of hot water. Spread a little icing over the top of each biscuit and place half a cherry on each. Leave until set before serving.

2

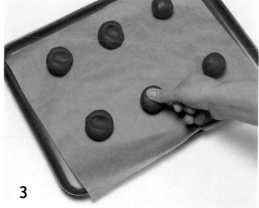

3

5

Chequered Biscuits

INGREDIENTS

Makes 20

150 g/5 oz butter
75 g/3 oz icing sugar
pinch of salt
200 g/7 oz plain flour
25 g/1 oz cocoa powder
1 small egg white

FOOD FACT

Recipes for sweet biscuits and pastries often contain a pinch of salt. This helps to enhance the sweet flavour without making it savoury.

HELPFUL HINT

When baking biscuits, use a fish slice or spatula to transfer the cut-out biscuits from the work surface to the baking sheets. Use heavy-duty baking sheets that will not bend or warp in the oven. The nonstick silicone baking sheets that are now readily available are ideal for baking biscuits. Follow the manufacturers' instructions for oiling.

1 Preheat the oven to 190°C/375°F/Gas Mark 5, 10 minutes before baking. Lightly oil 3–4 baking sheets. Place the butter and icing sugar in a bowl and cream together until light and fluffy.

2 Add the salt, then gradually add the flour, beating well after each addition. Mix well to form a firm dough. Cut the dough in half and knead the cocoa powder into one half. Wrap both portions of dough separately in clingfilm and then leave to chill in the refrigerator for 2 hours.

3 Divide each piece of dough into 3 portions. Roll each portion of dough into a long roll and arrange these rolls on top of each other to form a chequerboard design, sealing them with egg white. Wrap in clingfilm and refrigerate for 1 hour.

4 Cut the dough into 5 mm/¼ inch thick slices, place on the baking sheets and bake in the preheated oven for 10–15 minutes. Remove from the oven, and leave to cool for a few minutes. Transfer to a wire rack and leave until cold before serving. Store in an airtight tin.

1

2

3

Honey & Chocolate Hearts

INGREDIENTS

Makes about 20

60 g/2½ oz caster sugar

15 g/½ oz butter

125 g/4 oz thick honey

1 small egg, beaten

pinch of salt

1 tbsp mixed peel or chopped
  glacé ginger

¼ tsp ground cinnamon

pinch of ground cloves

225 g/8 oz plain flour, sifted

½ tsp baking powder, sifted

75 g/3 oz milk chocolate

HELPFUL HINT

When cutting out the hearts start at the outside edge working into the centre, cutting out the biscuits as close as possible to minimise the wastage. Press the trimmings lightly together and and roll out once more. Discard any remaining dough as it will be tougher and give a heavier biscuit, which will break up easily.

1 Preheat the oven to 220°C/425°F/Gas Mark 7, 15 minutes before baking. Lightly oil 2 baking sheets. Heat the sugar, butter and honey together in a small saucepan until everything has melted and the mixture is smooth.

2 Remove from the heat and stir until slightly cooled, then add the beaten egg with the salt and beat well. Stir in the mixed peel or glacé ginger, ground cinnamon, ground cloves, the flour and the baking powder and mix well until a dough is formed. Wrap in clingfilm and chill in the refrigerator for 45 minutes.

3 Place the chilled dough on a lightly floured surface, roll out to about 5 mm/¼ inch thickness and cut out small heart shapes. Place onto the prepared baking sheets and bake in the preheated oven for 8–10 minutes. Remove from the oven and leave to cool slightly. Using a spatula, transfer to a wire rack until cold.

4 Melt the chocolate in a heatproof bowl set over a saucepan of simmering water. Alternatively, melt the chocolate in the microwave according to the manufacturer's instructions, until smooth. Dip one half of each biscuit in the melted chocolate. Leave to set before serving.

1

3

4

Chocolate Orange Biscuits

INGREDIENTS

Makes 30

100 g/3½ oz plain dark chocolate
125 g/4 oz butter
125 g/4 oz caster sugar
pinch of salt
1 medium egg, beaten
grated zest of 2 oranges
200 g/7 oz plain flour
1 tsp baking powder
125 g/4 oz icing sugar
1–2 tbsp orange juice

HELPFUL HINT

To get the maximum amount of juice from citrus fruits, heat the whole fruit in the microwave for about 40 seconds, then cool slightly before squeezing. alternatively, roll the fruit on the table, pressing lightly before squeezing out the juice. It is important to add the orange juice gradually to the icing mixture because you may not need all of it to obtain a spreadable consistency.

1 Preheat the oven to 200°C/400°F/Gas Mark 6, 15 minutes before baking. Lightly oil several baking sheets. Coarsely grate the chocolate and reserve. Beat the butter and sugar together until creamy. Add the salt, beaten egg and half the orange zest and beat again.

2 Sift the flour and baking powder, add to the bowl with the grated chocolate and beat to form a dough. Shape into a ball, wrap in clingfilm and chill in the refrigerator for 2 hours.

3 Roll the dough out on a lightly floured surface to 5 mm/¼ inch thickness and cut into 5 cm/2 inch rounds. Place the rounds on the prepared baking sheets, allowing room for expansion. Bake in the preheated oven for 10–12 minutes or until firm. Remove the biscuits from the oven and leave to cool slightly. Using a spatula, transfer to a wire rack and leave to cool.

4 Sift the icing sugar into a small bowl and stir in sufficient orange juice to make a smooth, spreadable icing. Spread the icing over the biscuits, leave until almost set, then sprinkle on the remaining grated orange zest before serving.

1

2

3

Rum & Chocolate Squares

INGREDIENTS

Makes 14–16

125 g/4 oz butter
100 g/3½ oz caster sugar
pinch of salt
2 medium egg yolks
225 g/8 oz plain flour
50 g/2 oz cornflour
¼ tsp baking powder
2 tbsp cocoa powder
1 tbsp rum

1 Preheat the oven to 190°C/350°F/Gas Mark 5, 10 minutes before baking. Lightly oil several baking sheets. Cream the butter, sugar and salt together in a large bowl until light and fluffy. Add the egg yolks and beat well until smooth.

2 Sift together 175 g/6 oz of the flour, the cornflour and the baking powder and add to the mixture and mix well with a wooden spoon until a smooth and soft dough is formed.

3 Halve the dough and knead the cocoa powder into one-half and the rum and the remaining plain flour into the other half. Place the 2 mixtures in 2 separate bowls, cover with clingfilm and chill in the refrigerator for 1 hour.

4 Roll out both pieces of dough separately on a well floured surface into 2 thin rectangles. Place one on top of the other, cut out squares approximately 5 cm/2 inch x 5 mm/¼ inch and place on the prepared baking sheets.

5 Bake in the preheated oven, half with the chocolate uppermost and the other half, rum side up, for 10–12 minutes or until firm. Remove from the oven and leave to cool slightly. Using a spatula, transfer to a wire rack and leave to cool, then serve.

TASTY TIP

If you prefer, you could substitute rum flavouring for the rum in this recipe. However, you would need to reduce the amount to about 1 teaspoon.

1

3

4

Chocolate Whirls

INGREDIENTS

Makes 20

125 g/4 oz soft margarine
75 g/3 oz unsalted butter, softened
75 g/3 oz icing sugar, sifted
75 g/3 oz plain dark chocolate, melted and cooled
15 g/½ oz cornflour, sifted
125 g/4 oz plain flour
125 g/4 oz self-raising flour

For the butter cream:
125 g/4 oz unsalted butter, softened
½ tsp vanilla essence
225 g/8 oz icing sugar, sifted

HELPFUL HINT

It is important that the fats are at room temperature and the flours are sifted. Do not put too much mixture into the piping bag. If liked, the butter cream can be replaced with whipped cream, but the whirls should be eaten on the day they are filled.

1   Preheat the oven to 180°C/350°F/Gas Mark 4, 10 minutes before baking. Lightly oil 2 baking sheets. Cream the margarine, butter and icing sugar together until the mixture is light and fluffy.

2   Stir the chocolate until smooth, then beat into the creamed mixture. Stir in the cornflour. Sift the flours together, then gradually add to the creamed mixture, a little at a time, beating well between each addition. Beat until the consistency is smooth and stiff enough for piping.

3   Put the mixture in a piping bag fitted with a large star nozzle and pipe 40 small whirls onto the prepared baking sheets.

4   Bake the whirls in the preheated oven for 12–15 minutes or until firm to the touch. Remove from the oven and leave to cool for about 2 minutes. Using a spatula, transfer the whirls to wire racks and leave to cool.

5   Meanwhile, make the butter cream. Cream the butter with the vanilla essence until soft. Gradually beat in the icing sugar and add a little cooled boiled water, if necessary, to give a smooth consistency.

6   When the whirls are cold, pipe or spread on the prepared butter cream, sandwich together and serve.

2

3

6

Chunky Chocolate Muffins

INGREDIENTS

Makes 7

50 g/2 oz plain dark chocolate,
  roughly chopped
50 g/2 oz light muscovado sugar
25 g/1 oz butter, melted
125 ml/4 fl oz milk, heated to room
  temperature
½ tsp vanilla essence
1 medium egg, lightly beaten
150 g/5 oz self-raising flour
½ tsp baking powder
pinch of salt
75 g/3 oz white chocolate, chopped
2 tsp icing sugar (optional)

HELPFUL HINT

Measuring dry ingredients when baking is very important, too much or too little of any ingredient can change the end result quite substantially. This applies especially to raising agents like baking powder. It is a good idea to invest in a set of cooks measuring spoons and remember to use either metric or Imperial measurements. Do not mix the two when weighing out the ingredients.

1 Preheat the oven to 200°C/400°F/Gas Mark 6, 15 minutes before baking. Line a muffin or deep bun tin tray with 7 paper muffin cases or oil the individual compartments well. Place the plain chocolate in a large heatproof bowl set over a saucepan of very hot water and stir occasionally until melted. Remove the bowl and leave to cool for a few minutes.

2 Stir the sugar and butter into the melted chocolate, then the milk, vanilla essence and egg. Sift in the flour, baking powder and salt together. Add the chopped white chocolate, then using a metal spoon, fold together quickly, taking care not to overmix.

3 Divide the mixture between the paper cases, piling it up in the centre. Bake on the centre shelf of the preheated oven for 20–25 minutes, or until well risen and firm to the touch.

4 Lightly dust the tops of the muffins with icing sugar as soon as they come out of the oven, if using. Leave the muffins in the tins for a few minutes, then transfer to a wire rack. Serve warm or cold.

1

2

3

Rich Chocolate Cup Cakes

INGREDIENTS

Makes 12

175 g/6 oz self-raising flour
25 g/1 oz cocoa powder
175 g/6 oz soft light brown sugar
75 g/3 oz butter, melted
2 medium eggs, lightly beaten
1 tsp vanilla essence
40 g/1½ oz maraschino cherries,
   drained and chopped

For the chocolate icing:

50 g/2 oz plain dark chocolate
25 g/1 oz unsalted butter
25 g/1 oz icing sugar, sifted

For the cherry icing:

125 g/4 oz icing sugar
7 g/¼ oz unsalted butter, melted
1 tsp syrup from the maraschino
   cherries
3 maraschino cherries, halved, to
   decorate

TASTY TIP

Do not expect the cakes to rise to the top of the cake cases; they should only come about three-quarters of the way up.

1   Preheat the oven to 180°C/350°F/Gas Mark 4, 10 minutes before baking. Line a 12 hole muffin or deep bun tin tray with paper muffin cases. Sift the flour and cocoa powder into a bowl. Stir in the sugar, then add the melted butter, eggs and vanilla essence. Beat together with a wooden spoon for 3 minutes or until well blended.

2   Divide half the mixture between 6 of the paper cases. Dry the cherries thoroughly on absorbent kitchen paper, then fold into the remaining mixture and spoon into the rest of the paper cases.

3   Bake on the shelf above the centre of the preheated oven for 20 minutes, or until a skewer inserted into the centre of a cake comes out clean. Transfer to a wire rack and leave to cool.

4   For the chocolate icing, melt the chocolate and butter in a heatproof bowl set over a saucepan of hot water. Remove from the heat and leave to cool for 3 minutes, stirring occasionally. Stir in the icing sugar. Spoon over the 6 plain chocolate cakes and leave to set.

5   For the cherry icing, sift the icing sugar into a bowl and stir in 1 tablespoon of boiling water, the butter and cherry syrup. Spoon the icing over the remaining 6 cakes, decorate each with a halved cherry and leave to set.

1

3

4

Chocolate Chelsea Buns

INGREDIENTS

Makes 12

75 g/3 oz dried pears, finely chopped
1 tbsp apple or orange juice
225 g/8 oz strong plain flour
1 tsp ground cinnamon
½ tsp salt
40 g/1½ oz butter
1½ tsp easy-blend dried yeast
125 ml/4 fl oz warm milk
1 medium egg, lightly beaten
75 g/3 oz plain dark chocolate, chopped
3 tbsp maple syrup

1 Preheat the oven to 190°C/375°F/Gas Mark 5, 10 minutes before baking. Lightly oil an 18 cm/7 inch square tin. Place the pears in a bowl with the fruit juice, stir then cover and leave to soak while making the dough.

2 Sift the flour, cinnamon and salt into a bowl, rub in 25 g/1 oz of the butter then stir in the yeast and make a well in the middle. Add the milk and egg and mix to a soft dough. Knead on a floured surface for 10 minutes, until smooth and elastic, then place in a bowl. Cover with clingfilm and leave in a warm place to rise for 1 hour or until doubled in size.

3 Turn out on a lightly floured surface and knead the dough lightly before rolling out to a rectangle, about 30.5 x 23 cm/12 x 9 inches. Melt the remaining butter and brush over. Spoon the pears and chocolate evenly over the dough leaving a 2.5 cm/1 inch border, then roll up tightly, starting at a long edge. Cut into 12 equal slices, then place, cut-side up in the tin. Cover and leave to rise for 25 minutes, or until doubled in size.

4 Bake on the centre shelf of the preheated oven for 30 minutes, or until well risen and golden brown. Cover with tinfoil after 20 minutes, if the filling is starting to brown too much.

5 Brush with the maple syrup while hot, then leave in the tin for 10 minutes to cool slightly. Turn out onto a wire rack and leave to cool. Separate the buns and serve warm.

TASTY TIP

As an alternative replace the pears with an equal weight of chopped hazelnuts or almonds.

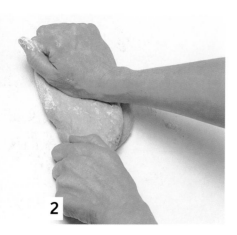

2

3

5

Chocolate Pecan Traybake

INGREDIENTS

Makes 12

175 g/6 oz butter
75 g/3 oz icing sugar, sifted
175 g/6 oz plain flour
25 g/1 oz self-raising flour
25 g/1 oz cocoa powder

For the pecan topping:

75 g/3 oz butter
50 g/2 oz light muscovado sugar
2 tbsp golden syrup
2 tbsp milk
1 tsp vanilla essence
2 medium eggs, lightly beaten
125 g/4 oz pecan halves

HELPFUL HINT

When a recipe calls for butter or margarine, the solid block variety (not the soft tub alternative, which has had air beaten in) must be used. Low-fat spreads break down on heating and, as they contain a large proportion of water, the end result will not be correct and the cake or tart will be disappointing.

1 Preheat the oven to 180°C/350°F/Gas Mark 4, 10 minutes before baking. Lightly oil and line a 28 x 18 x 2.5 cm/11 x 7 x 1 inch cake tin with nonstick baking parchment. Beat the butter and sugar together until light and fluffy. Sift in the flours and cocoa powder and mix together to form a soft dough.

2 Press the mixture evenly over the base of the prepared tin. Prick all over with a fork, then bake on the shelf above the centre of the preheated oven for 15 minutes.

3 Put the butter, sugar, golden syrup, milk and vanilla essence in a small saucepan and heat gently until melted. Remove from the heat and leave to cool for a few minutes, then stir in the eggs and pour over the base. Sprinkle with the nuts.

4 Bake in the preheated oven for 25 minutes or until dark golden brown, but still slightly soft. Leave to cool in the tin. When cool, carefully remove from the tin, then cut into 12 squares and serve. Store in an airtight container.

2

3

4

Moist Mocha & Coconut Cake

INGREDIENTS

Makes 9 squares

3 tbsp ground coffee
5 tbsp hot milk
75 g/3 oz butter
175 g/6 oz golden syrup
25 g/1 oz soft light brown sugar
40 g/1½ oz desiccated coconut
150 g/5 oz plain flour
25 g/1 oz cocoa powder
½ tsp bicarbonate of soda
2 medium eggs, lightly beaten
2 chocolate flakes, to decorate

For the coffee icing:

225 g/8 oz icing sugar, sifted
125 g/4 oz butter, softened

1 Preheat the oven to 170°C/325°F/Gas Mark 3, 10 minutes before baking. Lightly oil and line a deep 20.5 cm/8 inch square tin with nonstick baking parchment. Place the ground coffee in a small bowl and pour over the hot milk. Leave to infuse for 5 minutes, then strain through a tea-strainer or a sieve lined with muslin. You will end up with about 4 tablespoons of liquid. Reserve.

2 Put the butter, golden syrup, sugar and coconut in a small heavy-based saucepan and heat gently until the butter has melted and the sugar dissolved. Sift the flour, cocoa powder and bicarbonate of soda together and stir into the melted mixture with the eggs and 3 tablespoons of the coffee-infused milk.

3 Pour the mixture into the prepared tin. Bake on the centre shelf of the preheated oven for 45 minutes, or until the cake is well risen and firm to the touch. Leave in the tin for 10 minutes to cool slightly, then turn out onto a wire rack to cool completely.

4 For the icing, gradually add the icing sugar to the softened butter and beat together until mixed. Add the remaining 1 tablespoon of coffee-infused milk and beat until light and fluffy.

5 Carefully spread the coffee icing over the top of the cake, then cut into 9 squares. Decorate each square with a small piece of chocolate flake and serve.

HELPFUL HINT

It is important to use a very fine strainer to remove as much of the coffee as possible or the cake will have an unpleasant gritty texture.

2

3

5

Chocolate Walnut Squares

INGREDIENTS

Makes 24

125 g/4 oz butter

150 g/5 oz plain dark chocolate,
  broken into squares

450 g/1 lb caster sugar

½ tsp vanilla essence

200 g/7 oz plain flour

75 g/3 oz self-raising flour

50 g/2 oz cocoa powder

225 g/8 oz mayonnaise, at room
  temperature

For the chocolate glaze:

125 g/4 oz plain dark chocolate,
  broken into squares

40 g/1½ oz unsalted butter

24 walnut halves

1 tbsp icing sugar for dusting

TASTY TIP

Mayonnaise is used in this recipe instead of eggs. Make sure you use a plain rather than a flavoured mayonnaise.

1 Preheat the oven to 170°C/325°F/Gas Mark 3, 10 minutes before baking. Oil and line a 28 x 18 x 2.5 cm/11 x 7 x 1 inch cake tin with nonstick baking parchment. Place the butter, chocolate, sugar, vanilla essence and 225 ml/8 fl oz of cold water in a heavy-based saucepan. Heat gently, stirring occasionally, until the chocolate and butter have melted, but do not allow to boil.

2 Sift the flours and cocoa powder into a large bowl and make a well in the centre. Add the mayonnaise and about one-third of the chocolate mixture and beat until smooth. Gradually beat in the remaining chocolate mixture.

3 Pour into the prepared tin and bake on the centre shelf of the preheated oven for 1 hour, or until slightly risen and firm to the touch. Place the tin on a wire rack and leave to cool. Remove the cake from the tin and peel off the parchment paper.

4 To make the chocolate glaze, place the chocolate and butter in a small saucepan with 1 tablespoon of water and heat very gently, stirring occasionally until melted and smooth. Leave to cool until the chocolate has thickened, then spread evenly over the cake. Chill the cake in the refrigerator for about 5 minutes, then mark into 24 squares.

5 Lightly dust the walnut halves with a little icing sugar and place one on the top of each square. Cut into pieces and store in an airtight container until ready to serve.

1

2

4

Indulgent Chocolate Squares

INGREDIENTS

Makes 16

350 g/12 oz plain dark chocolate
175 g/6 oz butter, softened
175 g/6 oz soft light brown sugar
175 g/6 oz ground almonds
6 large eggs, separated
3 tbsp cocoa powder, sifted
75 g/3 oz fresh brown breadcrumbs
125 ml/4 fl oz double cream
50 g/2 oz white chocolate, chopped
50 g/2 oz milk chocolate, chopped
few freshly sliced strawberries,
  to decorate

1. Preheat the oven to 180°C/350°F/Gas Mark 4, 10 minutes before baking. Oil and line a deep 20.5 cm/8 inch square cake tin with nonstick baking parchment. Melt 225 g/8 oz of the dark chocolate in a heatproof bowl set over a saucepan of almost boiling water. Stir until smooth, then leave until just cool, but not beginning to set.

2. Beat the butter and sugar until light and fluffy. Stir in the melted chocolate, ground almonds, egg yolks, cocoa powder and breadcrumbs. Whisk the egg whites until stiff peaks form, then stir a large spoonful into the chocolate mixture. Gently fold in the rest, then pour the mixture into the prepared tin.

3. Bake on the centre shelf in the preheated oven for 1¼ hours, or until firm, covering the top with tinfoil after 45 minutes, to prevent it over-browning. Leave in the tin for 20 minutes, then turn out onto a wire rack and leave to cool.

4. Melt the remaining 125 g/4 oz plain chocolate with the cream in a heatproof bowl set over a saucepan of almost boiling water, stirring occasionally. Leave to cool for 20 minutes or until thickened slightly.

5. Spread the topping over the cake. Scatter over the white and milk chocolate and leave to set. Cut into 16 squares and serve decorated with a few freshly sliced strawberries, then serve.

HELPFUL HINT

To prevent the tinfoil from coming off the top of the tin, especially in a fan assisted oven, fold the tinfoil around the edge, rather than simply laying it on top.

2   2

5

Fruit & Nut Refrigerator Fingers

INGREDIENTS

Makes 12

14 pink and white marshmallows

75 g/3 oz luxury dried mixed fruit

25 g/1 oz candied orange peel, chopped

75 g/3 oz glacé cherries, quartered

75 g/3 oz walnuts, chopped

1 tbsp brandy

175 g/6 oz digestive biscuits, crushed

225 g/8 oz plain dark chocolate

125 g/4 oz unsalted butter

1 tbsp icing sugar, for dusting, optional

1 Lightly oil and line the base of a 18 cm/7 inch tin with nonstick baking parchment. Using oiled kitchen scissors, snip each marshmallow into 4 or 5 pieces over a bowl. Add the dried mixed fruit, orange peel, cherries and walnuts to the bowl. Sprinkle with the brandy and stir together. Add the crushed biscuits and stir until mixed.

2 Break the chocolate into squares and put in a heatproof bowl with the butter set over a saucepan of almost boiling water. Stir occasionally until melted, then remove from the heat. Pour the melted chocolate mixture over the dry ingredients and mix together well. Spoon into the prepared tin, pressing down firmly.

3 Chill in the refrigerator for 15 minutes, then mark into 12 fingers using a sharp knife. Chill in the refrigerator for a further 1 hour or until set. Turn out of the tin, remove the lining paper and cut into fingers. Dust with icing sugar before serving.

HELPFUL HINT

Why not try storing nuts in the freezer? Stored this way, whole nuts will keep for 3 years, shelled nuts for 1 year and ground nuts, such as ground almonds, for 3 months. Whole nuts will crack far easier when frozen, as their shells are far more brittle.

1

1

2

All-in-one Chocolate Fudge Cakes

INGREDIENTS

Makes 15 squares

175 g/6 oz soft dark brown sugar
175 g/6 oz butter, softened
150 g/5 oz self-raising flour
25 g/1 oz cocoa powder
½ tsp baking powder
pinch of salt
3 medium eggs, lightly beaten
1 tbsp golden syrup

For the fudge topping:

75 g/3 oz granulated sugar
150 ml/¼ pint evaporated milk
175 g/6 oz plain dark chocolate,
   roughly chopped
40 g/1½ oz unsalted butter, softened
125 g/4 oz soft fudge sweets, finely
   chopped

1 Preheat the oven to 180°C/350°F/Gas Mark 4, 10 minutes before baking. Oil and line a 28 x 18 x 2.5 cm/ 11 x 7 x 1 inch cake tin with nonstick baking parchment.

2 Place the soft brown sugar and butter in a bowl and sift in the flour, cocoa powder, baking powder and salt. Add the eggs and golden syrup, then beat with an electric whisk for 2 minutes, before adding 2 tablespoons of warm water and beating for a further 1 minute.

3 Turn the mixture into the prepared tin and level the top with the back of a spoon. Bake on the centre shelf of the preheated oven for 30 minutes, or until firm to the touch. Turn the cake out onto a wire rack and leave to cool before removing the baking parchment.

4 To make the topping, gently heat the sugar and evaporated milk in a saucepan, stirring frequently, until the sugar has dissolved. Bring the mixture to the boil and simmer for 6 minutes, without stirring.

5 Remove the mixture from the heat. Add the chocolate and butter and stir until melted and blended. Pour into a bowl and chill in the refrigerator for 1–2 hours or until thickened. Spread the topping over the cake, then sprinkle with the chopped fudge. Cut the cake into 15 squares before serving.

TASTY TIP

Use a mixture of fudge sweets for the topping on this cake, including chocolate, vanilla and toffee flavours.

2

3

5

Triple Chocolate Brownies

INGREDIENTS

Makes 15

350 g/12 oz plain dark chocolate, broken into pieces
225 g/8 oz butter, cubed
225 g/8 oz castor sugar
3 large eggs, lightly beaten
1 tsp vanilla essence
2 tbsp very strong black coffee
100 g/3½ oz self-raising flour
125 g/4 oz pecans, roughly chopped
75 g/3 oz white chocolate, roughly chopped
75 g/3 oz milk chocolate, roughly chopped

FOOD FACT

Brownies have a high proportion of sugar, giving the brownie its distinctive crusty topping. Underneath, the rich, gooey texture is produced by the small amount of flour used in comparison to the rest of ingredients.

TASTY TIP

Take care not to overcook; the outside crust should be crisp and the centre of the brownies moist and gooey.

1   Preheat the oven to 190°C/375°F/Gas Mark 5, 10 minutes before baking. Oil and line a 28 x 18 x 2.5 cm/11 x 7 x 1 inch cake tin with nonstick baking parchment. Place the plain chocolate in a heatproof bowl with the butter set over a saucepan of almost boiling water and stir occasionally until melted. Remove from the heat and leave until just cool, but not beginning to set.

2   Place the caster sugar, eggs, vanilla essence and coffee in a large bowl and beat together until smooth. Gradually beat in the chocolate mixture. Sift the flour into the chocolate mixture. Add the pecans and the white and milk chocolate and gently fold in until mixed thoroughly.

3   Spoon the mixture into the prepared tin and level the top. Bake on the centre shelf of the preheated oven for 45 minutes, or until just firm to the touch in the centre and crusty on top. Leave to cool in the tin, then turn out onto a wire rack. Trim off the crusty edges and cut into 15 squares. Store in an airtight container.

1

2

2

Chocolate Florentines

INGREDIENTS

Makes 20

125 g/4 oz butter or margarine

125 g/4 oz soft light brown sugar

1 tbsp double cream

50 g/2 oz blanched almonds,
   roughly chopped

50 g/2 oz hazelnuts,
   roughly chopped

75 g/3 oz sultanas

50 g/2 oz glacé cherries,
   roughly chopped

50 g/2 oz plain, dark chocolate,
   roughly chopped or broken

50 g/2 oz milk chocolate, roughly
   chopped or broken

50 g/2 oz white chocolate, roughly
   chopped or broken

TASTY TIP

Rich and fruity, these Florentines rely on their raw ingredients, so try to use a good-quality chocolate and natural glacé cherries, which have a fruitier taste and are more natural in colour.

1 Preheat the oven to 180°C/350°F/Gas Mark 4, 10 minutes before baking. Lightly oil a baking sheet.

2 Melt the butter or margarine with the sugar and double cream in a small saucepan over a very low heat. Do not boil.

3 Remove from the heat and stir in the almonds, hazelnuts, sultanas and cherries.

4 Drop teaspoonfuls of the mixture on to the baking sheet. Transfer to the preheated oven and bake for 10 minutes, until golden.

5 Leave the biscuits to cool on the baking sheet for about 5 minutes, then carefully transfer to a wire rack to cool.

6 Melt the plain, milk and white chocolates in separate bowls, either in the microwave following the manufacturers' instructions or in a small bowl, placed over a saucepan of gently simmering water.

7 Spread one-third of the biscuits with the plain chocolate, one-third with the milk chocolate and one-third with the white chocolate.

8 Mark out wavy lines on the chocolate when almost set with the tines of a fork. Or dip some of the biscuits in chocolate to half coat and serve.

3

5

7

Ginger Snaps

INGREDIENTS

Makes 40

300 g/11 oz butter or
  margarine, softened
225 g/8 oz soft light brown sugar
75 g/3 oz black treacle
1 medium egg
400 g/14 oz plain flour
2 tsp bicarbonate of soda
½ tsp salt
1 tsp ground ginger
1 tsp ground cloves
1 tsp ground cinnamon
50 g/2 oz granulated sugar

TASTY TIP

Ginger snaps are great biscuits to use in other recipes. Try crushing them, mixing with melted butter and using as the base for a cheesecake.

TASTY TIP

Ginger snaps are also delicious roughly broken up and added to home-made ice cream – particularly ginger or chocolate ice cream, as they have light, honeycomb textures.

1   Preheat the oven to 190°C/375°F/Gas Mark 5, 10 minutes before baking. Lightly oil a baking sheet.

2   Cream together the butter or margarine and the sugar until light and fluffy.

3   Warm the treacle in the microwave for 30–40 seconds, then add gradually to the butter mixture with the egg. Beat until combined well.

4   In a separate bowl, sift the flour, bicarbonate of soda, salt, ground ginger, ground cloves and ground cinnamon. Add to the butter mixture and mix together to form a firm dough.

5   Chill in the refrigerator for 1 hour. Shape the dough into small balls and roll in the granulated sugar. Place well apart on the oiled baking sheet.

6   Sprinkle the baking sheet with a little water and transfer to the preheated oven.

7   Bake for 12 minutes, until golden and crisp. Transfer to a wire rack to cool and serve

3

4

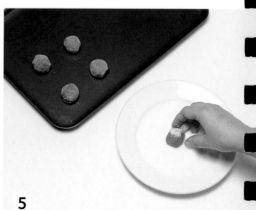

5

Oatmeal Raisin Cookies

INGREDIENTS

Makes 24

175 g/6 oz plain flour

150 g/5 oz rolled oats

1 tsp ground ginger

½ tsp baking powder

½ tsp bicarbonate of soda

125 g/4 oz soft light-brown sugar

50 g/2 oz raisins

1 medium egg, lightly beaten

150 ml/¼ pint vegetable or
sunflower oil

4 tbsp milk

1 Preheat the oven to 200°C/400°F/Gas Mark 6, 15 minutes before baking. Lightly oil a baking sheet.

2 Mix together the flour, oats, ground ginger, baking powder, bicarbonate of soda, sugar and the raisins in a large bowl.

3 In another bowl, mix the egg, oil and milk together. Make a well in the centre of the dry ingredients and pour in the egg mixture.

4 Mix the mixture together well with either a fork or a wooden spoon to make a soft but not sticky dough.

5 Place spoonfuls of the dough well apart on the oiled baking sheet and flatten the tops down slightly with the tines of a fork.

6 Transfer the biscuits to the preheated oven and bake for 10–12 minutes until golden.

7 Remove from the oven, leave to cool for 2–3 minutes, then transfer the biscuits to a wire rack to cool. Serve when cold or otherwise store in an airtight tin.

FOOD FACT

This dough can be made, wrapped in clingfilm then stored in the refrigerator for up to 1 week before baking. When ready to bake, simply cut off the dough and bake as above.

2

3

5

Almond Macaroons

INGREDIENTS

Makes 12

rice paper
125 g/4 oz caster sugar
50 g/2 oz ground almonds
1 tsp ground rice
2–3 drops almond essence
1 medium egg white
8 blanched almonds, halved

1 Preheat the oven to 150°C/300°F/Gas Mark 2, 10 minutes before baking. Line a baking sheet with the rice paper.

2 Mix the caster sugar, ground almonds, ground rice and almond essence together and reserve.

3 Whisk the egg white until stiff then gently fold in the caster sugar mixture with a metal spoon or rubber spatula.

4 Mix to form a stiff but not sticky paste. (If the mixture is very sticky, add a little extra ground almonds.)

5 Place small spoonfuls of the mixture, about the size of an apricot, well apart on the rice paper.

6 Place a half-blanched almond in the centre of each. Place in the preheated oven and bake for 25 minutes, or until just pale golden.

7 Remove the biscuits from the oven and leave to cool for a few minutes on the baking sheet. Cut or tear the rice paper around the macaroons to release them. Once cold, serve or otherwise store them in an airtight tin.

TASTY TIP

Rice paper is an edible paper made from the pith of the Chinese tree. These macaroons are deliciously chewy and are fantastic when broken up and sprinkled in desserts such as trifles. Serve with cream and tart fresh fruits such as raspberries.

2

3

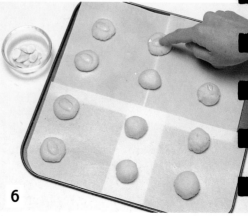

6

Pumpkin Cookies with Brown Butter Glaze

INGREDIENTS

Makes 48

125 g/4 oz butter, softened
150 g/5 oz plain flour
175 g/6 oz soft light brown sugar,
  lightly packed
225 g/8 oz canned pumpkin or
  cooked pumpkin
1 medium egg, beaten
2 tsp ground cinnamon
2½ tsp vanilla essence
½ tsp baking powder
½ tsp bicarbonate of soda
½ tsp freshly grated nutmeg
125 g/4 oz wholemeal flour
75 g/3 oz pecans, roughly chopped
100 g/3½ oz raisins
50 g/2 oz unsalted butter
225 g/8 oz icing sugar
2 tbsp milk

HELPFUL HINT

To cook pumpkin, slice off the top
and scrape out the seeds. Cut the
pumpkin vertically into quarters
and remove the dark orange skin
with a potato peeler. Cut the flesh
into chunks and steam or
microwave until tender. Purée to
use in the above recipe.

1   Preheat the oven to 190°C/375°F/Gas Mark 5, 10 minutes before
    baking. Lightly oil a baking sheet and reserve.

2   Using an electric mixer, beat the butter until light and fluffy. Add
    the flour, sugar, pumpkin, beaten egg and beat with the mixer until
    mixed well.

3   Stir in the ground cinnamon, 1 teaspoon of the vanilla essence and
    then sift in the baking powder, bicarbonate of soda and grated
    nutmeg. Beat the mixture until combined well, scraping down the
    sides of the bowl.

4   Add the wholemeal flour, chopped nuts and raisins to the mixture
    and fold in with a metal spoon or rubber spatula until mixed
    thoroughly together.

5   Place teaspoonfuls about 5 cm/2 inches apart on to the baking
    sheet. Bake in the pre-heated oven for 10–12 minutes, or until the
    cookie edges are firm.

6   Remove the biscuits from the oven and leave to cool on a wire rack.
    Meanwhile, melt the butter in a small saucepan over a medium
    heat, until pale and just turning golden brown.

7   Remove from the heat. Add the sugar, remaining vanilla essence
    and milk, stirring. Drizzle over the cooled cookies and serve.

3

5

7

Spiced Palmier Biscuits with Apple Purée

INGREDIENTS

Makes 20

250 g/9 oz prepared puff pastry,
  thawed if frozen
40 g/1½ oz caster sugar
25 g/1 oz icing sugar
1 tsp ground cinnamon
¼ tsp ground ginger
¼ tsp freshly grated nutmeg
450 g/1 lb Bramley cooking apples,
  roughly chopped
50 g/2 oz sugar
25 g/1 oz raisins
25 g/1 oz dried cherries
zest of 1 orange
double cream, lightly whipped,
  to serve

FOOD FACT

Palmiers are so called as they are thought to resemble palm leaves – palmier being the French word for a palm tree. Palmiers are often served sandwiched together with whipped cream and jam.

1   Preheat the oven to 200°C/400°F/Gas Mark 6, 15 minutes before baking. Roll out the pastry on a lightly floured surface to form a 25.5 x 30.5 cm/10 x 12 inch rectangle. Trim the edges with a small sharp knife.

2   Sift together the caster sugar, icing sugar, cinnamon, ginger and nutmeg into a bowl. Generously dust both sides of the pastry sheet with about a quarter of the sugar mixture.

3   With a long edge facing the body, fold either side halfway towards the centre. Dust with a third of the remaining sugar mixture.

4   Fold each side again so that they almost meet in the centre and dust again with about half the remaining sugar mixture. Fold the 2 sides together down the centre of the pastry to give 6 layers altogether. Wrap the pastry in clingfilm and refrigerate for 1–2 hours until firm. Reserve the remaining spiced sugar.

5   Remove the pastry from the refrigerator, unwrap and roll in the remaining sugar to give a good coating all round. Using a sharp knife, cut the roll into about 20 thin slices. Place the cut side down on to a baking sheet and place in the pre-heated oven.

6   Cook for 10 minutes, turn the biscuits and cook for a further 5–10 minutes, or until golden and crisp. Remove from the oven and transfer to a wire rack. Allow to cool completely.

7   Meanwhile, combine the remaining ingredients in a saucepan. Cover and cook gently for 15 minutes until the apple is completely soft. Stir well and allow to cool. Serve the palmiers with a spoonful of the apple purée and a little of the whipped double cream.

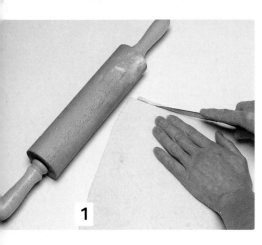

1

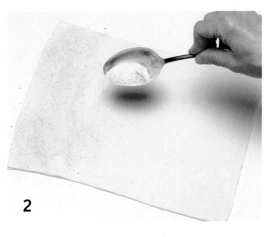

2

3

Peanut Butter Truffle Cookies

INGREDIENTS

Makes 18

125 g/4 oz plain dark chocolate

150 ml/¼ pint double cream

125 g/4 oz butter or
  margarine, softened

125 g/4 oz caster sugar

125 g/4 oz crunchy or smooth
  peanut butter

4 tbsp golden syrup

1 tbsp milk

225 g/8 oz plain flour

½ tsp bicarbonate of soda

HELPFUL HINT

Measure golden syrup either by warming a metal measuring spoon in boiling water, then dipping it into the syrup, or place the tin in a warm oven or saucepan half-filled with hot water.

1 Preheat the oven to 180°C/350°F/Gas Mark 4, 10 minutes before baking. Make the chocolate filling by breaking the chocolate into small pieces and placing in a heatproof bowl.

2 Put the double cream into a saucepan and heat to boiling point. Immediately pour over the chocolate.

3 Leave to stand for 1–2 minutes, then stir until smooth. Set aside to cool until firm enough to scoop. Do not refrigerate.

4 Lightly oil a baking sheet. Cream together the butter or margarine and the sugar until light and fluffy. Blend in the peanut butter, followed by the golden syrup and milk.

5 Sift together the flour and bicarbonate of soda. Add to the peanut butter mixture, mix well and knead until smooth.

6 Flatten 1–2 tablespoons of the cookie mixture on a chopping board.

7 Put a spoonful of the chocolate mixture into the centre of the cookie dough, then fold the dough around the chocolate to enclose completely.

8 Put the balls on to the baking sheet and flatten slightly. Bake in the preheated oven for 10–12 minutes until golden.

9 Remove from the oven and transfer to a wire rack to cool completely and serve.

2

4

7

Whipped Shortbread

INGREDIENTS

Makes 36

225 g/8 oz butter, softened
75 g/3 oz icing sugar
175 g/6 oz flour
hundreds and thousands
sugar strands
chocolate drops
silver balls
50 g/2 oz icing sugar
2–3 tsp lemon juice

HELPFUL HINT

Although these biscuits have the flavour of classic shortbread, the texture is much lighter. They literally melt in the mouth. These biscuits are great for children. However, for a smarter-looking biscuit which is more appealing to adults, spoon the mixture into a piping bag fitted with a large star nozzle and pipe the biscuits on to the baking sheet. Bake as above.

1 Preheat the oven to 180°C/350°F/Gas Mark 4, 10 minutes before baking. Lightly oil a baking sheet.

2 Cream the butter and icing sugar until fluffy. Gradually add the flour and continue beating for a further 2–3 minutes until it is smooth and light.

3 Roll into balls and place on a baking sheet. Cover half of the dough mixture with hundreds and thousands, sugar strands, chocolate drops or silver balls. Keep the other half plain.

4 Bake in the preheated oven for 6–8 minutes, until the bottoms are lightly browned. Remove from the oven and transfer to a wire rack to cool.

5 Sift the icing sugar into a small bowl. Add the lemon juice and blend until a smooth icing forms.

6 Using a small spoon swirl the icing over the cooled plain cookies. Decorate with either the extra hundreds and thousands, chocolate drops or silver balls and serve.

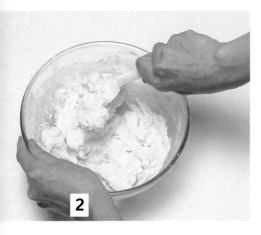

2

3

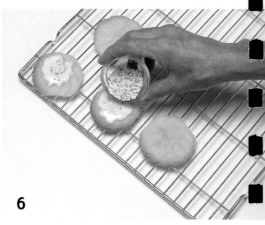

6

Oatmeal Coconut Cookies

INGREDIENTS

Makes 40

225 g/8 oz butter or margarine
125 g/4 oz soft light brown sugar
125 g/4 oz caster sugar
1 large egg, lightly beaten
1 tsp vanilla essence
225 g/8 oz plain flour
1 tsp baking powder
½ tsp bicarbonate of soda
125 g/4 oz rolled oats
75 g/3 oz desiccated coconut

1 Preheat the oven to 180°C/350°F/Gas Mark 4, 10 minutes before baking. Lightly oil a baking sheet.

2 Cream together the butter or margarine and sugars until light and fluffy.

3 Gradually stir in the egg and vanilla essence and beat until well blended.

4 Sift together the flour, baking powder and bicarbonate of soda in another bowl.

5 Add to the butter and sugar mixture and beat together until smooth. Fold in the rolled oats and coconut with a metal spoon or rubber spatula.

6 Roll heaped teaspoonfuls of the mixture into balls and place on the baking sheet about 5 cm/2 inches apart and flatten each ball slightly with the heel of the hand.

7 Transfer to the preheated oven and bake for 12–15 minutes, until just golden.

8 Remove from the oven and transfer the biscuits to a wire rack to completely cool and serve.

HELPFUL HINT

The raising agent in this recipe, bicarbonate of soda, lightens the texture of these biscuits, resulting in a crisp yet melting result. These biscuits will last for 3–4 days if stored in an airtight tin or jar.

3

5

6

Chocolate Biscuit Bars

INGREDIENTS

Makes 20 slices

50 g/2 oz sultanas
3–4 tbsp brandy (optional)
100 g/3½ oz plain dark chocolate
125 g/4 oz unsalted butter
2 tbsp golden syrup
90 ml/3 fl oz double cream
6 digestive biscuits,
   roughly crushed
50 g/2 oz shelled pistachio nuts,
   toasted and roughly chopped
50 g/2 oz blanched almonds, toasted
   and roughly chopped
50 g/2 oz glacé cherries,
   roughly chopped
grated zest of 1 orange
cocoa powder, sifted

1 Lightly oil a 20.5 cm/8 inch square tin and line with clingfilm.

2 Place the sultanas into a small bowl and pour over the brandy, if using. Leave to soak for 20–30 minutes.

3 Meanwhile, break the chocolate into small pieces and put into a heatproof bowl.

4 Place the bowl over a saucepan of simmering water, making sure that the bottom of the bowl does not touch the water.

5 Leave the chocolate until melted, stirring occasionally. Remove from the heat.

6 Add the butter, golden syrup and double cream to a small saucepan and heat until the butter has melted.

7 Remove the saucepan from the heat and add the melted chocolate, biscuits, nuts, cherries, orange zest, sultanas and the brandy mixture.

8 Mix thoroughly and pour into the prepared tin. Smooth the top and chill in the refrigerator for at least 4 hours, or until firm.

9 Turn out the cake and remove the clingfilm. Dust liberally with the cocoa powder then cut into bars to serve. Store lightly covered in the refrigerator.

HELPFUL HINT

You may find these bars slice more easily if you heat the knife first. Run the blade of the knife under hot water and wipe dry with a clean tea towel, then slice.

5

7

9

Apple & Cinnamon Crumble Bars

INGREDIENTS

Makes 16

450 g/1 lb Bramley cooking apples,
   roughly chopped
50 g/2 oz raisins
50 g/2 oz caster sugar
1 tsp ground cinnamon
zest of 1 lemon
200 g/7 oz plain flour
250 g/9 oz soft light brown sugar
½ tsp bicarbonate of soda
150 g/5 oz rolled oats
150 g/5 oz butter, melted
crème fraîche or whipped cream,
   to serve

TASTY TIP

The apple filling in this recipe is very similar to American apple butter. To make apple butter, cook the filling in step 2 for a further 30 minutes over a very low heat, stirring often. When reduced to one-third of its original volume (it should be quite dark) then it is ready. It is delicious spread on toast.

1 Preheat the oven to 190°C/375°F/Gas Mark 5, 10 minutes before baking. Place the apples, raisins, sugar, cinnamon and lemon zest into a saucepan over a low heat.

2 Cover and cook for about 15 minutes, stirring occasionally, until the apple is cooked through. Remove the cover, stir well to break up the apple completely with a wooden spoon.

3 Cook for a further 15–30 minutes over a very low heat until reduced, thickened and slightly darkened. Allow to cool. Lightly oil and line a 20.5 cm/8 inch square cake tin with greaseproof or baking paper.

4 Mix together the flour, sugar, bicarbonate of soda, rolled oats and butter until combined well and crumbly.

5 Spread half of the flour mixture into the bottom of the prepared tin and press down. Pour over the apple mixture.

6 Sprinkle over the remaining flour mixture and press down lightly. Bake in the preheated oven for 30–35 minutes, until golden brown.

7 Remove from the oven and allow to cool before cutting into slices. Serve the bars warm or cold with crème fraîche or whipped cream.

Lemon Bars

INGREDIENTS

Makes 24

175 g/6 oz flour
125 g/4 oz butter
50 g/2 oz granulated sugar
200 g/7 oz caster sugar
2 tbsp flour
$\frac{1}{2}$ tsp baking powder
$\frac{1}{4}$ tsp salt
2 medium eggs, lightly beaten
juice and finely grated rind of
  1 lemon
sifted icing sugar, to decorate

FOOD FACT

Baking Powder is a chemically prepared raising agent consisting of cream of tartar and bicarbonate of soda, which is then mixed with a dried starch or flour. It is very important to measure accurately, otherwise the mixture could either not rise, or rise too quickly and then collapse, and give a sour taste to the dish.

1 Preheat the oven to 170°C/325°F/Gas Mark 3, 10 minutes before baking. Lightly oil and line a 20.5 cm/8 inch square cake tin with greaseproof or baking paper.

2 Rub together the flour and butter until the mixture resembles breadcrumbs. Stir in the granulated sugar and mix.

3 Turn the mixture into the prepared tin and press down firmly. Bake in the preheated oven for 20 minutes, until pale golden.

4 Meanwhile, in a food processor, mix together the caster sugar, flour, baking powder, salt, eggs, lemon juice and rind until smooth. Pour over the prepared base.

5 Transfer to the preheated oven and bake for a further 20–25 minutes, until nearly set but still a bit wobbly in the centre. Remove from the oven and cool in the tin on a wire rack.

6 Dust with icing sugar and cut into squares. Serve cold or store in an airtight tin.

Pecan Caramel Millionaire's Shortbread

INGREDIENTS

Makes 20

125 g/4 oz butter, softened
2 tbsp smooth peanut butter
75 g/3 oz caster sugar
75 g/3 oz cornflour
175 g/6 oz plain flour

For the topping:

200 g/7 oz caster sugar
125 g/4 oz butter
2 tbsp golden syrup
75 g/3 oz liquid glucose
75 ml/3 fl oz water
400 g can sweetened
  condensed milk
175 g/6 oz pecans,
  roughly chopped
75 g/3 oz plain dark chocolate
1 tbsp butter

TASTY TIP

Any type of nut can be used in this recipe. Why not try replacing the pecans with a variety of chopped walnuts, almonds and brazil nuts?

1 Preheat the oven to 180°C/350°F/Gas Mark 4, 10 minutes before baking. Lightly oil and line an 18 cm x 28 cm/7 x 11 inch tin with greaseproof or baking paper.

2 Cream together the butter, peanut butter and sugar until light. Sift in the cornflour and flour together and mix in to make a smooth dough.

3 Press the mixture into the prepared tin and prick all over with a fork. Bake in the preheated oven for 20 minutes, until just golden. Remove from the oven.

4 Meanwhile, for the topping, combine the sugar, butter, golden syrup, glucose, water and milk in a heavy-based saucepan. Stir constantly over a low heat without boiling until the sugar has dissolved. Increase the heat, boil steadily, stirring constantly, for about 10 minutes until the mixture turns a golden caramel colour.

5 Remove the saucepan from the heat and add the pecans. Pour over the shortbread base immediately. Allow to cool, then refrigerate for at least 1 hour.

6 Break the chocolate into small pieces and put into a heatproof bowl with the butter. Place over a saucepan of barely simmering water, ensuring that the bowl does not come into contact with the water. Leave until melted, then stir together well.

7 Remove the shortbread from the refrigerator and pour the chocolate evenly over the top, spreading thinly to cover. Leave to set, cut into squares and serve.

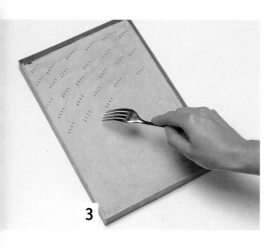

3

5

7

Fruit & Nut Flapjacks

INGREDIENTS

Makes 12

75 g/3 oz butter or margarine
125 g/4 oz soft light brown sugar
3 tbsp golden syrup
50 g/2 oz raisins
50 g/2 oz walnuts,
    roughly chopped
175 g/6 oz rolled oats
50 g/2 oz icing sugar
1–1½ tbsp lemon juice

TASTY TIP

These flapjacks are packed with energy, but why not increase the nutritional value by adding a few tablespoons of seeds, such as sesame, sunflower and pumpkin seeds, then add some chopped up ready-to-eat fruit such as apricot, pineapple or mango. You can also add chocolate cooking chips, chopped glacé fruits as well as currants and sultanas.

1 Preheat the oven to 180°C/350°F/Gas Mark 4, 10 minutes before baking. Lightly oil a 23 cm/9 inch square cake tin.

2 Melt the butter or margarine with the sugar and syrup in a small saucepan over a low heat. Remove from the heat.

3 Stir the raisins, walnuts and oats into the syrup mixture and mix together well.

4 Spoon evenly into the prepared tin and press down well. Transfer to the preheated oven and bake for 20–25 minutes.

5 Remove from the oven and leave to cool in the tin. Cut into bars while still warm.

6 Sift the icing sugar into a small bowl then gradually beat in the lemon juice a little at a time to form a thin icing.

7 Place into an icing bag fitted with a writing nozzle then pipe thin lines over the flapjacks. Allow to cool and serve.

2

3

7

Chocolate Fudge Brownies

INGREDIENTS

Makes 16

125 g/4 oz butter
175 g/6 oz plain dark chocolate,
   roughly chopped or broken
225 g/8 oz caster sugar
2 tsp vanilla essence
2 medium eggs, lightly beaten
150 g/5 oz plain flour
175 g/6 oz icing sugar
2 tbsp cocoa powder
15 g/½ oz butter

FOOD FACT

Chocolate is obtained from the bean of the cacao tree and was introduced to Europe in the 16th Century. It is available in many different forms from cocoa powder to couverture, which is the best chocolate to use for cooking as it has a high cocoa butter content and melts very smoothly.

1 Preheat the oven to 180°C/350°F/Gas Mark 4, 10 minutes before baking. Lightly oil and line a 20.5 cm/8 inch square cake tin with greaseproof or baking paper.

2 Slowly melt the butter and chocolate together in a heatproof bowl set over a saucepan of simmering water. Transfer the mixture to a large bowl.

3 Stir in the sugar and vanilla essence, then stir in the eggs. Sift over the flour and fold together well with a metal spoon or rubber spatula. Pour into the prepared tin.

4 Transfer to the preheated oven and bake for 30 minutes until just set. Remove the cooked mixture from the oven and leave to cool in the tin before turning it out on to a wire rack.

5 Sift the icing sugar and cocoa powder into a small bowl and make a well in the centre.

6 Place the butter in the well then gradually add about 2 tablespoons of hot water. Mix to form a smooth spreadable icing.

7 Pour the icing over the cooked mixture. Allow the icing to set before cutting into squares. Serve the brownies when they are cold.

2

3

5

Chocolate Nut Brownies

INGREDIENTS

Makes 16

125 g/4 oz butter

150 g/5 oz soft light brown sugar,
firmly packed

50 g/2 oz plain dark chocolate,
roughly chopped or broken

2 tbsp smooth peanut butter

2 medium eggs

50 g/2 oz unsalted roasted peanuts,
finely chopped

100 g/3½ oz self-raising flour

For the topping:

125 g/4 oz plain dark chocolate,
roughly chopped or broken

50 ml/2 fl oz soured cream

TASTY TIP

For those with a really sweet tooth, replace the plain dark chocolate used for the topping with white chocolate. As with plain dark chocolate, buy a good quality white chocolate and take care when melting; it burns very easily in the microwave.

1 Preheat the oven to 180°C/350°F/Gas Mark 4, 10 minutes before baking. Lightly oil and line a 20.5 cm/8 inch square cake tin with greaseproof or baking paper.

2 Combine the butter, sugar and chocolate in a small saucepan and heat gently until the sugar and chocolate have melted, stirring constantly. Reserve and cool slightly.

3 Mix together the peanut butter, eggs and peanuts in a large bowl.

4 Stir in the cooled chocolate mixture. Sift in the flour and fold together with a metal spoon or rubber spatula until combined.

5 Pour into the prepared tin and bake in the preheated oven for about 30 minutes, or until just firm.

6 Cool for 5 minutes in the tin before turning out on to a wire rack to cool.

7 To make the topping, melt the chocolate in a heatproof bowl over a saucepan of simmering water, making sure that the base of the bowl does not touch the water.

8 Cool slightly, then stir in the soured cream until smooth and glossy. Spread over the brownies, refrigerate until set, then cut into squares. Serve the brownies cold.

4

5

8

Gingerbread

INGREDIENTS

Cuts into 8 slices

175 g/6 oz butter or margarine

225 g/8 oz black treacle

50 g/2 oz dark muscovado sugar

350 g/12 oz plain flour

2 tsp ground ginger

150 ml/¼ pint milk, warmed

2 medium eggs

1 tsp bicarbonate of soda

1 piece of stem ginger in syrup

1 tbsp stem ginger syrup

FOOD FACT

There are many different types of gingerbread, ranging in colour from deep rich dark brown to light golden. This is due to the type of treacle and the amount of bicarbonate of soda used. One well-known gingerbread from Yorkshire is Parkin which uses both golden syrup and black treacle.

1 Preheat the oven to 150°C/300°C/Gas Mark 2, 10 minutes before baking. Lightly oil and line the base of a 20.5 cm/8 inch deep round cake tin with greaseproof or baking paper.

2 In a saucepan gently heat the butter or margarine, black treacle and sugar, stirring occasionally until the butter melts. Leave to cool slightly.

3 Sift the flour and ground ginger into a large bowl.

4 Make a well in the centre, then pour in the treacle mixture. Reserve 1 tablespoon of the milk, then pour the rest into the treacle mixture. Stir together lightly until mixed.

5 Beat the eggs together, then stir into the mixture.

6 Dissolve the bicarbonate of soda in the remaining 1 tablespoon of warmed milk and add to the mixture.

7 Beat the mixture until well mixed and free of lumps.

8 Pour into the prepared tin and bake in the preheated oven for 1 hour, or until well risen and a skewer inserted into the centre comes out clean.

9 Cool in the tin, then remove. Slice the stem ginger into thin slivers and sprinkle over the cake. Drizzle with the syrup and serve.

2

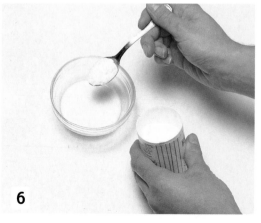

6

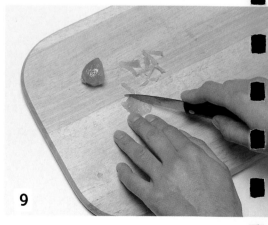

9

Jammy Buns

INGREDIENTS

Makes 12

175 g/6 oz plain flour
175 g/6 oz wholemeal flour
2 tsp baking powder
150 g/5 oz butter or margarine
125 g/4 oz golden caster sugar
50 g/2 oz dried cranberries
1 large egg, beaten
1 tbsp milk
4–5 tbsp seedless raspberry jam

TASTY TIP

In this recipe any type of jam can be used. However, look for one with a high-fruit content. Alternatively replace the jam with a fruit compote. Simply boil some fruit with a little sugar and water, then leave to cool before placing inside the buns.

1 Preheat the oven to 190°C/375°F/Gas Mark 5, 10 minutes before baking. Lightly oil a large baking sheet.

2 Sift the flours and baking powder together into a large bowl, then tip in the grains remaining in the sieve.

3 Cut the butter or margarine into small pieces. (It is easier to do this when the butter is in the flour as it helps stop the butter from sticking to the knife.)

4 Rub the butter into the flours until it resembles coarse breadcrumbs. Stir in the sugar and cranberries.

5 Using a round bladed knife stir in the beaten egg and milk. Mix to form a firm dough. Divide the mixture into 12 and roll into balls.

6 Place the dough balls on the baking tray, leaving enough space for expansion. Press the thumb into the centre of each ball making a small hollow.

7 Spoon a little of the jam in each hollow. Pinch lightly to seal the tops.

8 Bake in the preheated oven for 20–25 minutes, or until golden brown. Cool on a wire rack and serve.

4

6

7

Baked Puddings

The scrumptious tarts, pies and puddings in this section are great for sharing with friends and family. Impress and indulge your guests with the Triple Chocolate Cheesecake, the Lattice Treacle Tart or the Crunchy Rhubarb Crumble. Don't forget to save yourself a slice!

Chocolate Brioche Bake

INGREDIENTS

Serves 6

200 g/7 oz plain dark chocolate,
  broken into pieces

75 g/3 oz unsalted butter

225 g/8 oz brioche, sliced

1 tsp pure orange oil or 1 tbsp grated
  orange rind

½ tsp freshly grated nutmeg

3 medium eggs, beaten

25 g/1 oz golden caster sugar

600 ml/1 pint milk

cocoa powder and icing sugar
  for dusting

1   Preheat the oven to 180°C/350°F/Gas Mark 4, 10 minutes before baking. Lightly oil or butter a 1.7 litre/3 pint ovenproof dish. Melt the chocolate with 25 g/1 oz of the butter in a heatproof bowl set over a saucepan of simmering water. Stir until smooth.

2   Arrange half of the sliced brioche in the ovenproof dish, overlapping the slices slightly, then pour over half of the melted chocolate. Repeat the layers, finishing with a layer of chocolate.

3   Melt the remaining butter in a saucepan. Remove from the heat and stir in the orange oil or rind, the nutmeg and the beaten eggs. Continuing to stir, add the sugar and finally the milk. Beat thoroughly and pour over the brioche. Leave to stand for 30 minutes before baking.

4   Bake on the centre shelf in the preheated oven for 45 minutes, or until the custard is set and the topping is golden brown. Leave to stand for 5 minutes, then dust with cocoa powder and icing sugar. Serve warm.

FOOD FACT

Brioche is a type of French bread, enriched with eggs, butter and sugar. It is available as a large round loaf, as a plait or in a long loaf shape and also as individual buns. Any type is suitable for this recipe.

1

2

3

Chocolate Roulade

INGREDIENTS

Serves 8

150 g/5 oz golden caster sugar
5 medium eggs, separated
50 g/2 oz cocoa powder

For the filling:

300 ml/½ pint double cream
3 tbsp whisky
50 g/2 oz creamed coconut, chilled
2 tbsp icing sugar
coarsely shredded coconut, toasted

1　Preheat the oven to 180°C/350°F/Gas Mark 4, 10 minutes before baking. Oil and line a 33 x 23 cm/13 x 9 inch Swiss roll tin with a single sheet of nonstick baking parchment. Dust a large sheet of baking parchment with 2 tablespoons of the caster sugar.

2　Place the egg yolks in a bowl with the remaining sugar, set over a saucepan of gently simmering water and whisk until pale and thick. Sift the cocoa powder into the mixture and carefully fold in.

3　Whisk the egg whites in a clean, grease-free bowl until soft peaks form. Gently add 1 tablespoon of the whisked egg whites into the chocolate mixture then fold in the remaining whites. Spoon the mixture onto the prepared tin, smoothing the mixture into the corners. Bake in the preheated oven for 20–25 minutes, or until risen and springy to the touch.

4　Turn the cooked roulade out onto the sugar-dusted baking parchment and carefully peel off the lining paper. Cover with a clean damp tea towel and leave to cool.

5　To make the filling, pour the cream and whisky into a bowl and whisk until the cream holds its shape. Grate in the chilled creamed coconut, add the icing sugar and gently stir in. Uncover the roulade and spoon about three-quarters of coconut cream on the roulade and roll up. Spoon the remaining cream on the top and sprinkle with the coconut, then serve.

HELPFUL HINT

Take care when rolling up the roulade in this recipe as it can break up quite easily.

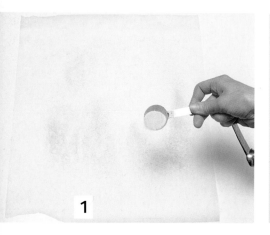

1

3

4

Triple Chocolate Cheesecake

INGREDIENTS

Serves 6

For the base:
150 g/5 oz digestive biscuits, crushed
50 g/2 oz butter, melted

For the cheesecake:
75 g/3 oz white chocolate, roughly
  chopped
300 ml/½ pint double cream
50 g/2 oz caster sugar
3 medium eggs, beaten
400 g/14 oz full fat soft cream cheese
2 tbsp cornflour
75 g/3 oz plain dark chocolate,
  roughly chopped
75 g/3 oz milk chocolate, roughly
  chopped
fromage frais, to serve

HELPFUL HINT

Leaving the cheesecake to cool in the oven helps to prevent cracks from forming on the top. However, do not worry if the top does crack – it will not affect the flavour of the cheesecake.

1 Preheat the oven to 180°C/350°F/Gas Mark 4, 10 minutes before baking. Lightly oil a 23 x 7.5 cm/9 x 3 inch springform tin.

2 To make the base, mix together the crushed biscuits and melted butter. Press into the base of the tin and leave to set. Chill in the refrigerator.

3 Place the white chocolate and cream in a small heavy-based saucepan and heat gently until the chocolate has melted. Stir until smooth and reserve.

4 Beat the sugar and eggs together until light and creamy in colour, add the cream cheese and beat until the mixture is smooth and free from lumps.

5 Stir the reserved white chocolate cream together with the cornflour into the soft cream cheese mixture.

6 Add the dark and milk chocolate to the soft cream cheese mixture and mix lightly together until blended.

7 Spoon over the chilled base, place on a baking sheet and bake in the preheated oven for 1 hour.

8 Switch off the heat, open the oven door and leave the cheesecake to cool in the oven. Chill in the refrigerator for at least 6 hours before removing the cheesecake from the tin. Cut into slices and transfer to serving plates. Serve with fromage frais.

2

4

6

Baked Lemon & Sultana Cheesecake

INGREDIENTS

Cuts into 10 slices

275 g/10 oz caster sugar

50 g/2 oz butter

50 g/2 oz self-raising flour

½ level tsp baking powder

5 large eggs

450 g/1 lb cream cheese

40 g/1½ oz plain flour

grated rind of 1 lemon

3 tbsp fresh lemon juice

150 ml/¼ pint crème fraîche

75 g/3 oz sultanas

To decorate:

1 tbsp icing sugar

fresh blackcurrants or blueberries

mint leaves

TASTY TIP

Vary the flavour by adding a little freshly grated nutmeg and ½ teaspoon of ground cinnamon to the base in step 2. Add a little of both spices to the icing sugar before sprinkling.

1 Preheat the oven to 170°C/325°F/Gas Mark 3. Oil a 20.5 cm/8 inch loose-bottomed round cake tin with non-stick baking paper.

2 Beat 50 g/2 oz of the sugar and the butter together until light and creamy, then stir in the self-raising flour, baking powder and 1 egg.

3 Mix lightly together until well blended. Spoon into the prepared tin and spread the mixture over the base. Separate the 4 remaining eggs and reserve.

4 Blend the cheese in a food processor until soft. Gradually add the eggs yolks and sugar and blend until smooth. Turn into a bowl and stir in the rest of the flour, lemon rind and juice.

5 Mix lightly before adding the crème fraîche and sultanas, stirring well.

6 Whisk the egg whites until stiff, fold into the cheese mixture and pour into the tin. Tap lightly on the surface to remove any air bubbles. Bake in the preheated oven for about 1 hour, or until golden and firm.

7 Cover lightly if browning too much. Switch the oven off and leave in the oven to cool for 2–3 hours.

8 Remove the cheesecake from the oven and when completely cold remove from the tin. Sprinkle with the icing sugar, decorate with the blackcurrants or blueberries and mint leaves and serve.

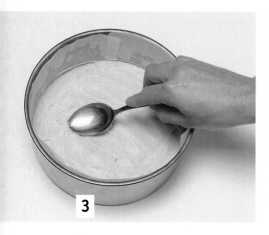

3

4

5

Crunchy Rhubarb Crumble

INGREDIENTS

Serves 6

125 g/4 oz plain flour
50 g/2 oz softened butter
50 g/2 oz rolled oats
50 g/2 oz demerara sugar
1 tbsp sesame seeds
½ tsp ground cinnamon
450 g/1 lb fresh rhubarb
50 g/2 oz caster sugar
custard or cream, to serve

TASTY TIP

To make homemade custard, pour 600 ml/1 pint of milk with a few drops of vanilla essence into a saucepan and bring to the boil. Remove from the heat and allow to cool. Meanwhile, whisk 5 egg yolks and 3 tablespoons of caster sugar together in a mixing bowl until thick and pale in colour. Add the milk, stir and strain into a heavy-based saucepan. Cook the custard on a low heat, stirring constantly until the consistency of double cream. Pour over the rhubarb crumble and serve.

1 Preheat the oven to 180°C/350°F/Gas Mark 4. Place the flour in a large bowl and cut the butter into cubes. Add to the flour and rub in with the fingertips until the mixture looks like fine breadcrumbs, or blend for a few seconds in a food processor.

2 Stir in the rolled oats, demerara sugar, sesame seeds and cinnamon. Mix well and reserve.

3 Prepare the rhubarb by removing the thick ends of the stalks and cut diagonally into 2.5 cm/1 inch chunks. Wash thoroughly and pat dry with a clean tea towel. Place the rhubarb in a 1.1 litre/2 pint pie dish.

4 Sprinkle the caster sugar over the rhubarb and top with the reserved crumble mixture. Level the top of the crumble so that all the fruit is well covered and press down firmly. If liked, sprinkle the top with a little extra caster sugar.

5 Place on a baking sheet and bake in the preheated oven for 40–50 minutes, or until the fruit is soft and the topping is golden brown. Sprinkle the pudding with some more caster sugar and serve hot with custard or cream.

2

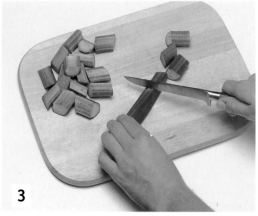

3

4

Iced Bakewell Tart

INGREDIENTS

Cuts into 8 slices

For the rich pastry:
175 g/6 oz plain flour
pinch of salt
60 g/2½ oz butter, cut into
  small pieces
50 g/2 oz white vegetable fat,
  cut into small pieces
2 small egg yolks, beaten

For the filling:
125 g/4 oz butter, melted
125 g/4 oz caster sugar
125 g/4 oz ground almonds
2 large eggs, beaten
few drops of almond essence
2 tbsp seedless raspberry jam

For the icing:
125 g/4 oz icing sugar, sifted
6–8 tsp fresh lemon juice
25 g/1 oz toasted flaked almonds

1 Preheat the oven to 200°C/400°F/Gas Mark 6. Place the flour and salt in a bowl, rub in the butter and vegetable fat until the mixture resembles breadcrumbs. Alternatively, blend quickly, in short bursts in a food processor.

2 Add the eggs with sufficient water to make a soft, pliable dough. Knead lightly on a floured board then chill in the refrigerator for about 30 minutes. Roll out the pastry and use to line a 23 cm/9 inch loose-bottomed flan tin.

3 For the filling, mix together the melted butter, sugar, almonds and beaten eggs and add a few drops of almond essence. Spread the base of the pastry case with the raspberry jam and spoon over the egg mixture.

4 Bake in the preheated oven for about 30 minutes, or until the filling is firm and golden brown. Remove from the oven and allow to cool completely.

5 When the tart is cold make the icing by mixing together the icing sugar and lemon juice, a little at a time, until the icing is smooth and of a spreadable consistency.

6 Spread the icing over the tart, leave to set for 2–3 minutes and sprinkle with the almonds. Chill in the refrigerator for about 10 minutes and serve.

2

3

6

Queen of Puddings

INGREDIENTS

Serves 4

75 g/3 oz fresh
  white breadcrumbs
25 g/1 oz granulated sugar
450 ml/³/₄ pint full-cream milk
25 g/1 oz butter
grated rind of 1 small lemon
2 medium eggs, separated
2 tbsp seedless raspberry jam
50 g/2 oz caster sugar

HELPFUL HINT

When whisking egg whites it is imperative that the bowl is completely clean and free of any grease. To ensure that the meringue does not collapse, whisk the egg whites until stiff. Gradually add the sugar, a spoonful at a time, whisking well between each addition. Place in the oven immediately after all of the sugar has been added.

1 Preheat the oven to 170°C/325°F/Gas Mark 3. Oil a 900 ml/1¹/₂ pint ovenproof baking dish and reserve.

2 Mix the breadcrumbs and sugar together in a bowl.

3 Pour the milk into a small saucepan and heat gently with the butter and lemon rind until the butter has melted.

4 Allow the mixture to cool a little, then pour over the breadcrumbs. Stir well and leave to soak for 30 minutes.

5 Whisk the egg yolks into the cooled breadcrumb mixture and pour into the prepared dish.

6 Place the dish on a baking sheet and bake in the preheated oven for about 30 minutes, or until firm and set. Remove from the oven.

7 Allow to cool slightly, then spread the jam over the pudding. Whisk the egg whites until stiff and standing in peaks.

8 Gently fold in the caster sugar with a metal spoon or rubber spatula. Pile the meringue over the top of the pudding.

9 Return the dish to the oven for a further 25–30 minutes, or until the meringue is crisp and just slightly coloured. Serve hot or cold.

3

5

7

Chocolate Sponge Pudding with Fudge Sauce

INGREDIENTS

Serves 4

75 g/3 oz butter
75 g/3 oz caster sugar
50 g/2 oz plain dark
 chocolate, melted
50 g/2 oz self-raising flour
25 g/1 oz drinking chocolate
1 large egg
1 tbsp icing sugar, to dust
crème fraîche, to serve

For the fudge sauce:

50 g/2 oz soft light brown sugar
1 tbsp cocoa powder
40 g/1½ oz pecan nuts,
 roughly chopped
25 g/1 oz caster sugar
300 ml/½ pint hot, strong
 black coffee

TASTY TIP

Try placing 6 halved and stoned fresh red plums in the base of the dish before adding the prepared chocolate sponge.

1 Preheat the oven to 170°C/325°F/Gas Mark 3. Oil a 900 ml/1½ pint pie dish.

2 Cream the butter and the sugar together in a large bowl until light and fluffy.

3 Stir in the melted chocolate, flour, drinking chocolate and egg and mix together.

4 Turn the mixture into the prepared dish and level the surface.

5 To make the fudge sauce, blend the brown sugar, cocoa powder and pecan nuts together and sprinkle evenly over the top of the pudding.

6 Stir the caster sugar into the hot black coffee until it has dissolved.

7 Carefully pour the coffee over the top of the pudding.

8 Bake in the preheated oven for 50–60 minutes, until the top is firm to touch. There will now be a rich sauce underneath the sponge.

9 Remove from the oven, dust with icing sugar and serve hot with crème fraîche.

3

5

7

Eve's Pudding

INGREDIENTS

Serves 6

450 g/1 lb cooking apples
175 g/6 oz blackberries
75 g/3 oz demerara sugar
grated rind of 1 lemon
125 g/4 oz caster sugar
125 g/4 oz butter
few drops of vanilla essence
2 medium eggs, beaten
125 g/4 oz self-raising flour
1 tbsp icing sugar
ready-made custard, to serve

FOOD FACT

Eve's pudding is a classic English pudding and has been popular since the early 20th century. At that time there were many different varieties of cooking apples grown throughout the country. Unfortunately, many of these apples have now disappeared.

1. Preheat the oven to 180°C/350°F/Gas Mark 4. Oil a 1.1 litre/2 pint baking dish.

2. Peel, core and slice the apples and place a layer in the base of the prepared dish.

3. Sprinkle over some of the blackberries, a little demerara sugar and lemon zest.

4. Continue to layer the apple and blackberries in this way until all the ingredients have been used.

5. Cream the sugar and butter together until light and fluffy.

6. Beat in the vanilla essence and then the eggs a little at a time, adding a spoonful of flour after each addition. Fold in the extra flour with a metal spoon or rubber spatula and mix well.

7. Spread the sponge mixture over the top of the fruit and level with the back of a spoon.

8. Place the dish on a baking sheet and bake in the preheated oven for 35–40 minutes, or until well risen and golden brown. (To test if the pudding is cooked, press the cooked sponge lightly with a clean finger – if it springs back the sponge is cooked.)

9. Dust the pudding with a little icing sugar and serve immediately with the custard.

3

6

7

Lemon & Apricot Pudding

INGREDIENTS

Serves 4

125 g/4 oz ready-to-eat
   dried apricots
3 tbsp orange juice, warmed
50 g/2 oz butter
125 g/4 oz caster sugar
juice and grated rind of 2 lemons
2 medium eggs
50 g/2 oz self-raising flour
300 ml/½ pint milk
custard or fresh cream, to serve

HELPFUL HINT

This pudding is cooked in a bain-marie to control the temperature around the dish – it needs to stay at just below boiling point. Bain-maries are ideal when cooking custards, sauces and other egg dishes. When using one, ensure that the water is kept topped up.

1   Preheat the oven to 180°C/350°F/Gas Mark 4. Oil a 1.1 litre/2 pint pie dish.

2   Soak the apricots in the orange juice for 10–15 minutes or until most of the juice has been absorbed, then place in the base of the pie dish.

3   Cream the butter and sugar together with the lemon rind until light and fluffy.

4   Separate the eggs. Beat the egg yolks into the creamed mixture with a spoonful of flour after each addition. Add the remaining flour and beat well until smooth.

5   Stir the milk and lemon juice into the creamed mixture. Whisk the egg whites in a grease-free mixing bowl until stiff and standing in peaks. Fold into the mixture using a metal spoon or rubber spatula.

6   Pour into the prepared dish and place in a baking tray filled with enough cold water to come halfway up the sides of the dish.

7   Bake in the preheated oven for about 45 minutes, or until the sponge is firm and golden brown. Remove from the oven. Serve immediately with the custard or fresh cream.

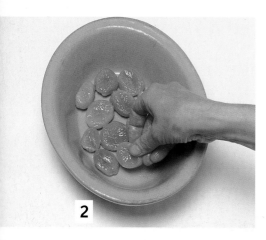

2

5

6

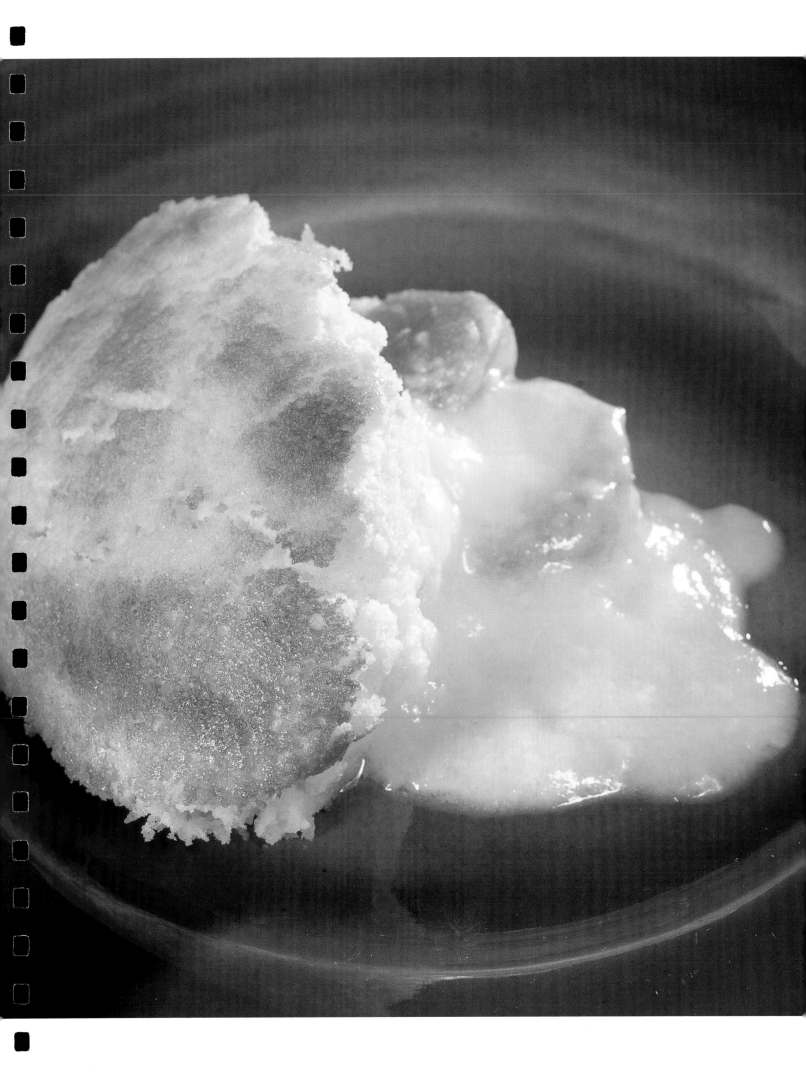

Rich Double-crust Plum Pie

INGREDIENTS

Serves 6

For the Pastry:
75 g/3 oz butter
75 g/3 oz white vegetable fat
225 g/8 oz plain flour
2 medium egg yolks

For the filling:
450 g/1 lb fresh plums,
   preferably Victoria
50 g/2 oz caster sugar
1 tbsp milk
a little extra caster sugar

HELPFUL HINT
As Victoria plums have only a short season, from August to September, it is best to use other varieties that have been imported. Alternatively, buy English plums in season. Halve, store and freeze them then use as required.

1 Preheat the oven to 200°C/400°F/Gas Mark 6. Make the pastry by rubbing the butter and white vegetable fat into the flour until it resembles fine breadcrumbs or blend in a food processor. Add the egg yolks and enough water to make a soft dough. Knead lightly, then wrap and leave in the refrigerator for about 30 minutes.

2 Meanwhile, prepare the fruit. Rinse and dry the plums, then cut in half and remove the stones. Slice the plums into chunks and cook in a saucepan with 25 g/1 oz of the sugar and 2 tablespoons of water for 5–7 minutes, or until slightly softened. Remove from the heat and add the remaining sugar to taste and allow to cool.

3 Roll out half the chilled pastry on a lightly floured surface and use to line the base and sides of a 1.1 litre/2 pint pie dish. Allow the pastry to hang over the edge of the dish. Spoon in the prepared plums.

4 Roll out the remaining pastry to use as the lid and brush the edge with a little water. Wrap the pastry around the rolling pin and place over the plums.

5 Press the edges together to seal and mark a decorative edge around the rim of the pastry by pinching with the thumb and forefinger or using the back of a fork.

6 Brush the lid with milk, and make a few slits in the top. Use any trimmings to decorate the top of the pie with pastry leaves. Place on a baking sheet and bake in the preheated oven for 30 minutes, or until golden brown. Sprinkle with a little caster sugar and serve hot or cold.

2

4

5

Baked Apple Dumplings

INGREDIENTS

Serves 4

225 g/8 oz self-raising flour
¼ tsp salt
125 g/4 oz shredded suet
4 medium cooking apples
4–6 tsp luxury mincemeat
1 medium egg white, beaten
2 tsp caster sugar
custard or vanilla sauce, to serve

TASTY TIP

To make vanilla sauce, blend 1½ tablespoons of cornflour with 3 tablespoons of milk to a smooth paste. Bring just under 300 ml/½ pint of milk to just below boiling point. Stir in the cornflour paste and cook over a gentle heat, stirring throughout until thickened and smooth. Remove from the heat and add 1 tablespoon of caster sugar, a knob of butter and ½ teaspoon of vanilla essence. Stir until the sugar and butter have melted, then serve.

1 Preheat the oven to 200°C/400°F/Gas Mark 6. Lightly oil a baking tray. Place the flour and salt in a bowl and stir in the suet.

2 Add just enough water to the mixture to mix to a soft but not sticky dough, using the fingertips.

3 Turn the dough on to a lightly floured board and knead lightly into a ball.

4 Divide the dough into 4 pieces and roll out each piece into a thin square, large enough to encase the apples.

5 Peel and core the apples and place 1 apple in the centre of each square of pastry.

6 Fill the centre of the apple with mincemeat, brush the edges of each pastry square with water and draw the corners up to meet over each apple.

7 Press the edges of the pastry firmly together and decorate with pastry leaves and shapes made from the extra pastry trimmings.

8 Place the apples on the prepared baking tray, brush with the egg white and sprinkle with the sugar.

9 Bake in the preheated oven for 30 minutes or until golden and the pastry and apples are cooked. Serve the dumplings hot with the custard or vanilla sauce.

2

6

7

Jam Roly Poly

INGREDIENTS

Serves 6

225 g/8 oz self-raising flour
¼ tsp salt
125 g/4 oz shredded suet
about 150 ml/¼ pint water
3 tbsp strawberry jam
1 tbsp milk, to glaze
1 tsp caster sugar
ready-made jam sauce, to serve

TASTY TIP

To make jam sauce, warm 4 tablespoons of jam such as seedless raspberry jam with 150 ml/¼ pint of water or orange juice. Stir until smooth. Blend 2 teaspoons of arrowroot with 1 tablespoon of water or juice to a smooth paste. Bring the jam mixture to almost boiling point, then stir in the blended arrowroot. Cook, stirring until the mixture thickens slightly and clears, then serve.

1. Preheat the oven to 200°C/400°F/Gas Mark 6. Make the pastry by sifting the flour and salt into a large bowl.

2. Add the suet and mix lightly, then add the water a little at a time and mix to form a soft and pliable dough. (Take care not to make the dough too wet.)

3. Turn the dough out on to a lightly floured board and knead gently until smooth.

4. Roll the dough out into a 23 cm/9 inch x 28 cm/11 inch rectangle.

5. Spread the jam over the pastry leaving a border of 1 cm/½ inch all round. Fold the border over the jam and brush the edges with water.

6. Lightly roll the rectangle up from one of the short sides, seal the top edge and press the ends together. (Do not roll the pudding up too tightly.)

7. Turn the pudding upside down on to a large piece of greaseproof paper large enough to come halfway up the sides. (If using non-stick paper, then oil lightly.)

8. Tie the ends of the paper, to make a boat-shaped paper case for the pudding to sit in and to leave plenty of room for the roly poly to expand.

9. Brush the pudding lightly with milk and sprinkle with the sugar. Bake in the preheated oven for 30–40 minutes, or until well risen and golden. Serve immediately with the jam sauce.

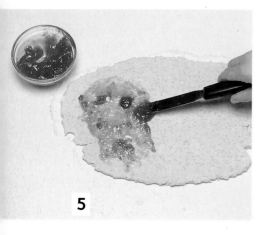

5

6

8

Egg Custard Tart

INGREDIENTS

Serves 6

Sweet pastry:
50 g/2 oz butter
50 g/2 oz white vegetable fat
175 g/6 oz plain flour
1 medium egg yolk, beaten
2 tsp caster sugar

For the filling:
300 ml/½ pint milk
2 medium eggs, plus
   1 medium egg yolk
25 g/1 oz caster sugar
½ tsp freshly grated nutmeg

HELPFUL HINT
Nowadays eggs are normally date stamped so it is possible to ensure that they are eaten when they are at their best. Another way to test if an egg is fresh is to place an uncooked egg in a bowl of water – if it lies at the bottom it is fresh; if it tilts it is older (use for frying or scrambling); if it floats, discard.

1   Preheat the oven to 200°C/400°F/Gas Mark 6. Oil a 20.5 cm/8 inch flan tin or dish.

2   Make the pastry by cutting the butter and vegetable fat into small cubes. Add to the flour in a large bowl and rub in, until the mixture resembles fine breadcrumbs.

3   Add the egg, sugar and enough water to form a soft and pliable dough. Turn on to a lightly floured board and knead. Wrap and chill in the refrigerator for 30 minutes.

4   Roll the pastry out on to a lightly floured surface or pastry board and use to line the oiled flan tin. Place in the refrigerator to reserve.

5   Warm the milk in a small saucepan. Briskly whisk together the eggs, egg yolk and caster sugar.

6   Pour the milk into the egg mixture and whisk until blended.

7   Strain through a sieve into the pastry case. Place the flan tin on a baking sheet.

8   Sprinkle the top of the tart with nutmeg and bake in the preheated oven for about 15 minutes.

9   Turn the oven down to 170°C/ 325°F/Gas Mark 3 and bake for a further 30 minutes, or until the custard has set. Serve hot or cold.

2

6

7

Golden Castle Pudding

INGREDIENTS

Serves 4–6

125 g/4 oz butter
125 g/4 oz caster sugar
a few drops of vanilla essence
2 medium eggs, beaten
125 g/4 oz self-raising flour
4 tbsp golden syrup
crème fraîche or ready-made custard, to serve

1 Preheat the oven to 180°C/350°F/Gas Mark 4. Lightly oil 4–6 individual pudding bowls and place a small circle of lightly oiled non-stick baking or greaseproof paper in the base of each one.

2 Place the butter and caster sugar in a large bowl, then beat together until the mixture is pale and creamy. Stir in the vanilla essence and gradually add the beaten eggs, a little at a time. Add a tablespoon of flour after each addition of egg and beat well.

3 When the mixture is smooth, add the remaining flour and fold in gently. Add a tablespoon of water and mix to form a soft mixture that will drop easily off a spoon.

4 Spoon enough mixture into each basin to come halfway up the tin, allowing enough space for the puddings to rise. Place on a baking sheet and bake in the preheated oven for about 25 minutes until firm and golden brown.

5 Allow the puddings to stand for 5 minutes. Discard the paper circle and turn out on to individual serving plates.

6 Warm the golden syrup in a small saucepan and pour a little over each pudding. Serve hot with the crème fraîche or custard.

HELPFUL HINT

For a change, make the traditional Castle Pudding by placing a spoonful of jam in the base of each basin. Top with the sponge and bake.

1

4

6

College Pudding

INGREDIENTS

Serves 4

125 g/4 oz shredded suet
125 g/4 oz fresh
  white breadcrumbs
50 g/2 oz sultanas
50 g/2 oz seedless raisins
½ tsp ground cinnamon
¼ tsp freshly grated nutmeg
¼ tsp mixed spice
50 g/2 oz caster sugar
½ tsp baking powder
2 medium eggs, beaten
orange zest, to garnish

TASTY TIP

Like many other suet puddings this recipe is relatively cheap to make. For extra fruitiness add some apple purée to the mixture. To make, peel, core and chop 1 cooking apple. Place in a saucepan with 25 g/1 oz of sugar and 4 tablespoons of water. Simmer until softened but not falling apart, then roughly mash. Add the purée to the mixture in step 3 and continue as before.

1 Preheat the oven to 180°C/350°F/Gas Mark 4. Lightly oil an ovenproof 900 ml/1½ pint ovenproof pudding basin and place a small circle of greaseproof paper in the base.

2 Mix the shredded suet and breadcrumbs together and rub lightly together with the fingertips to remove any lumps.

3 Stir in the dried fruit, spices, sugar and baking powder. Add the eggs and beat lightly together until the mixture is well blended and the fruit is evenly distributed.

4 Spoon the mixture into the prepared pudding basin and level the surface. Place on a baking tray and cover lightly with some greaseproof paper.

5 Bake in the preheated oven for 20 minutes, then remove the paper and continue to bake for a further 10–15 minutes, or until the top is firm.

6 When the pudding is cooked, remove from the oven and carefully turn out on to a warmed serving dish. Decorate with the orange zest and serve immediately.

2

3

4

Apple & Cinnamon Brown Betty

INGREDIENTS

Serves 4

450 g/1 lb cooking apples
50 g/2 oz caster sugar
finely grated rind of 1 lemon
125 g/4 oz fresh white breadcrumbs
125 g/4 oz demerara sugar
½ tsp ground cinnamon
25 g/1 oz butter

For the custard:

3 medium egg yolks
1 tbsp caster sugar
500 ml/1 pint milk
1 tbsp cornflour
few drops of vanilla essence

TASTY TIP

For a richer, more luxurious custard, substitute the milk in this recipe for double cream and increase the number of eggs yolks used to 4.

1   Preheat the oven to 180°C/350°F/Gas Mark 4. Lightly oil a 900 ml/1½ pint ovenproof dish. Peel, core and slice the apples and place in a saucepan with the caster sugar, lemon rind and 2 tablespoons of water. Simmer for 10–15 minutes or until tender.

2   Mix the breadcrumbs with the sugar and the cinnamon. Place half the sweetened apples in the base of the prepared dish and spoon over half of the crumb mixture. Place the remaining apples on top and cover with the rest of the crumb mixture.

3   Melt the butter and pour over the surface of the pudding. Cover the dish with non-stick baking paper and bake in the preheated oven for 20 minutes. Remove the paper and bake for a further 10–15 minutes, or until golden.

4   Meanwhile, make the custard by whisking the egg yolks and sugar together until creamy. Mix 1 tablespoon of the milk with the cornflour, until a paste forms and reserve.

5   Warm the rest of the milk until nearly boiling and pour over the egg mixture with the paste and vanilla essence.

6   Place the bowl over a saucepan of gently simmering water. Stir over the heat until thickened and can coat the back of a spoon. Strain into a jug and serve hot over the pudding.

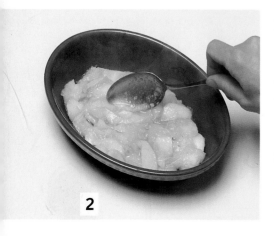

2

2

6

Lattice Treacle Tart

INGREDIENTS

Serves 4

For the pastry:
175 g/6 oz plain flour
40 g/1½ oz butter
40 g/1½ oz white vegetable fat

For the filling:
225 g/8 oz golden syrup
finely grated rind and juice
  of 1 lemon
75 g/3 oz fresh white breadcrumbs
1 small egg, beaten

1 Preheat the oven to 190°C/375°F/Gas Mark 5. Make the pastry by placing the flour, butter and white vegetable fat in a food processor. Blend in short sharp bursts until the mixture resembles fine breadcrumbs. Remove from the processor and place on a pastry board or in a large bowl.

2 Stir in enough cold water to make a dough and knead in a large bowl or on a floured surface until smooth and pliable.

3 Roll out the pastry and use to line a 20.5 cm/8 inch loose-bottomed fluted flan dish or tin. Reserve the pastry trimmings for decoration. Chill for 30 minutes.

4 Meanwhile, to make the filling, place the golden syrup in a saucepan and warm gently with the lemon rind and juice. Tip the breadcrumbs into the pastry case and pour the syrup mixture over the top.

5 Roll the pastry trimmings out on a lightly floured surface and cut into 6–8 thin strips. Lightly dampen the pastry edge of the tart, then place the strips across the filling in a lattice pattern. Brush the ends of the strips with water and seal to the edge of the tart. Brush a little beaten egg over the pastry and bake in the preheated oven for a 25 minutes, or until the filling is just set. Serve hot or cold.

TASTY TIP
Why not replace the breadcrumbs with the same amount of desiccated coconut?

2

4

5

Osborne Pudding

INGREDIENTS

Serves 4

8 slices of white bread
50 g/2 oz butter
2 tbsp marmalade
50 g/2 oz luxury mixed
   dried fruit
2 tbsp fresh orange juice
40 g/1½ oz caster sugar
2 large eggs
450 ml/¾ pint milk
150 ml/¼ pint whipping cream

For the marmalade sauce:

zest and juice of 1 orange
2 tbsp thick-cut
   orange marmalade
1 tbsp brandy (optional)
2 tsp cornflour

TASTY TIP

To make an orange sauce instead, omit the marmalade and add the juice of another 3 oranges and a squeeze of lemon juice to make 250 ml/9 fl oz. Follow the recipe as before but increase the cornflour to 1½ tablespoons.

1 Preheat the oven to 170°C/325°F/Gas Mark 3. Lightly oil a 1.1 litre/ 2 pint baking dish.

2 Remove the crusts from the bread and spread thickly with butter and marmalade. Cut the bread into small triangles.

3 Place half the bread in the base of the dish and sprinkle over the dried mixed fruit, 1 tablespoon of the orange juice and half the caster sugar.

4 Top with the remaining bread and marmalade, buttered side up and pour over the remaining orange juice. Sprinkle over the remaining caster sugar.

5 Whisk the eggs with the milk and cream and pour over the pudding. Reserve for about 30 minutes to allow the bread to absorb the liquid.

6 Place in a roasting tin and pour in enough boiling water to come halfway up the sides of the dish. Bake in the preheated oven for 50–60 minutes, or until the pudding is set and the top is crisp and golden.

7 Meanwhile, make the marmalade sauce. Heat the orange zest and juice with the marmalade and brandy if using.

8 Mix 1 tablespoon of water with the cornflour and mix together well.

9 Add to the saucepan and cook on a low heat, stirring until warmed through and thickened. Serve the pudding hot with the marmalade sauce.

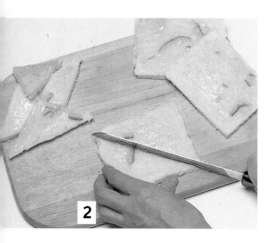

2

3

5

Chocolate Pecan Pie

INGREDIENTS

Cuts into 8–10 slices

225 g/8 oz prepared shortcrust pastry
200 g/7 oz pecan halves
125 g/4 oz plain dark chocolate, chopped
25 g/1 oz butter, diced
3 medium eggs
125 g/4 oz light brown sugar
175 ml/6 fl oz golden syrup
2 tsp vanilla essence
vanilla ice cream, to serve

HELPFUL HINT

Store chocolate in a cool, dark, dry place. The best temperature to store it at is 20°C/68°F – if any warmer the chocolate will sweat.

HELPFUL HINT

The pastry case in this recipe is not baked blind, but the pie does not become soggy because of the long cooking time, which allows the pastry to become crisp.

1 Preheat the oven to 180°C/350°F/Gas Mark 4, 10 minutes before baking. Roll the prepared pastry out on a lightly floured surface and use to line a 25.5 cm/10 inch pie plate. Roll the trimmings out and use to make a decorative edge around the pie, then chill in the refrigerator for 1 hour.

2 Reserve about 60 perfect pecan halves, or enough to cover the top of the pie, then coarsely chop the remainder and reserve. Melt the chocolate and butter in a small saucepan over a low heat or in the microwave and reserve.

3 Beat the eggs and brush the base and sides of the pastry with a little of the beaten egg. Beat the sugar, golden syrup and vanilla essence into the beaten eggs. Add the pecans, then beat in the chocolate mixture.

4 Pour the filling into the pastry case and arrange the reserved pecan halves in concentric circles over the top. Bake in the preheated oven for 45–55 minutes, or until the filling is well risen and just set. If the pastry edge begins to brown too quickly, cover with strips of tinfoil. Remove from the oven and serve with ice cream.

1

3

4

Pear & Chocolate Custard Tart

INGREDIENTS

Cuts into 6–8 slices

For the chocolate pastry:

125 g/4 oz unsalted butter, softened

60 g/2½ oz caster sugar

2 tsp vanilla essence

175 g/6 oz plain flour, sifted

40 g/1½ oz cocoa powder

whipped cream, to serve

For the filling:

125 g/4 oz plain dark chocolate, chopped

225 ml/8 fl oz whipping cream

50 g/2 oz caster sugar

1 large egg

1 large egg yolk

1 tbsp crème de cacao

3 ripe pears

HELPFUL HINT

The chocolate pastry is very soft so rolling it between sheets of clingfilm will make it much easier to handle without having to add a lot of extra flour.

1 Preheat the oven to 190°C/375°F/Gas Mark 5, 10 minutes before baking. To make the pastry, put the butter, sugar and vanilla essence into a food processor and blend until creamy. Add the flour and cocoa powder and process until a soft dough forms. Remove the dough, wrap in clingfilm and chill in the refrigerator for at least 1 hour.

2 Roll out the dough between 2 sheets of clingfilm to a 28 cm/11 inch round. Peel off the top sheet of clingfilm and invert the pastry round into a lightly oiled 23 cm/9 inch loose-based flan tin, easing the dough into the base and sides. Prick the base with a fork, then chill in the refrigerator for 1 hour.

3 Place a sheet of nonstick baking parchment and baking beans in the case and bake blind in the preheated oven for 10 minutes. Remove the parchment and beans and bake for a further 5 minutes. Remove and cool.

4 To make the filling, heat the chocolate, cream and half the sugar in a medium saucepan over a low heat, stirring until melted and smooth. Remove from the heat and cool slightly before beating in the egg, egg yolk and crème de cacao. Spread evenly over the pastry case base.

5 Peel the pears, then cut each pear in half and carefully remove the core. Cut each half crossways into thin slices and arrange over the custard, gently fanning the slices towards the centre and pressing into the chocolate custard. Bake in the oven for 10 minutes.

6 Reduce the oven temperature to 180°C/350°F/Gas Mark 4 and sprinkle the surface evenly with the remaining sugar. Bake in the oven for 20–25 minutes, or until the custard is set and the pears are tender and glazed. Remove from the oven and leave to cool slightly. Cut into slices, then serve with spoonfuls of whipped cream.

1

2

5

Caramelised Chocolate Tartlets

INGREDIENTS

Serves 6

350 g/12 oz ready-made shortcrust
  pastry, thawed if frozen
150 ml/¼ pint coconut milk
40 g/1½ oz demerara sugar
50 g/2 oz plain dark
  chocolate, melted
1 medium egg, beaten
few drops vanilla essence
1 small mango, peeled, stoned
  and sliced
1 small papaya, peeled, deseeded
  and chopped
1 star fruit, sliced
1 kiwi, peeled and sliced, or use fruits
  of your choice

1 Preheat the oven to 200°C/400°F/Gas Mark 6, 15 minutes before baking. Lightly oil 6 individual tartlet tins. Roll out the ready-made pastry on a lightly floured surface and use to line the oiled tins. Prick the bases and sides with a fork and line with nonstick baking parchment and baking beans. Bake blind for 10 minutes in the preheated oven, then remove from the oven and discard the baking beans and the baking parchment.

2 Reduce the oven temperature to 180°C/ 350°F/Gas Mark 4. Heat the coconut milk and 15 g/½ oz of the sugar in a heavy-based saucepan, stirring constantly until the sugar has dissolved. Remove the saucepan from the heat and leave to cool.

3 Stir the melted chocolate, the beaten egg and the vanilla essence into the cooled coconut milk. Stir until well mixed, then strain into the cooked pastry cases. Place on a baking sheet and bake in the oven for 25 minutes or until set. Remove and leave to cool, then chill in the refrigerator.

4 Preheat the grill, then arrange the fruits in a decorative pattern on the top of each tartlet. Sprinkle with the remaining demerara sugar and place the tartlets in the grill pan. Grill for 2 minutes or until the sugar bubbles and browns. Turn the tartlets, if necessary and take care not to burn the sugar. Remove from the grill and leave to cool before serving.

HELPFUL HINT

Before grilling, you may find it useful to cover the edges of the pastry with tinfoil to prevent it burning under the hot grill.

1

3

4

Topsy Turvy Pudding

INGREDIENTS

Serves 6

For the topping:
175 g/6 oz demerara sugar
2 oranges

For the sponge:
175 g/6 oz butter, softened
175 g/6 oz caster sugar
3 medium eggs, beaten
175 g/6 oz self-raising flour, sifted
50 g/2 oz plain dark chocolate, melted
grated rind of 1 orange
25 g/1 oz cocoa powder, sifted
custard or soured cream, to serve

HELPFUL HINT
When making the caramel in step 1, make sure the sugar has completely dissolved and that no sugar remains clinging to the side of the pan, otherwise the caramel will crystallise.

1 Preheat the oven to 180°C/350°F/Gas Mark 4, 10 minutes before baking. Lightly oil a 20.5 cm/8 inch deep round loose-based cake tin. Place the demerara sugar and 3 tablespoons of water in a small heavy-based saucepan and heat gently until the sugar has dissolved. Swirl the saucepan or stir with a clean wooden spoon to ensure the sugar has dissolved, then bring to the boil and boil rapidly until a golden caramel is formed. Pour into the base of the tin and leave to cool.

2 For the sponge, cream the butter and sugar together until light and fluffy. Gradually beat in the eggs a little at a time, beating well between each addition. Add a spoonful of flour after each addition to prevent the mixture curdling. Add the melted chocolate and then stir well. Fold in the orange rind, self-raising flour and sifted cocoa powder and mix well.

3 Remove the peel from both oranges taking care to remove as much of the pith as possible. Thinly slice the peel into strips and then slice the oranges. Arrange the peel and then the orange slices over the caramel. Top with the sponge mixture and level the top.

4 Place the tin on a baking sheet and bake in the preheated oven for 40–45 minutes or until well risen, golden brown and an inserted skewer comes out clean. Remove from the oven, leave for about 5 minutes, invert onto a serving plate and sprinkle with cocoa powder. Serve with either custard or soured cream.

Fruity Chocolate Bread Pudding

INGREDIENTS

Serves 4

175 g/6 oz plain dark chocolate
1 small fruit loaf
125 g/4 oz ready-to-eat dried apricots,
 roughly chopped
450 ml/³/₄ pint single cream
300 ml/¹/₂ pint milk
1 tbsp caster sugar
3 medium eggs
3 tbsp demerara sugar, for sprinkling

1 Preheat the oven to 180°C/350°F/Gas Mark 4, 10 minutes before cooking. Lightly butter a shallow ovenproof dish. Break the chocolate into small pieces, then place in a heatproof bowl set over a saucepan of gently simmering water. Heat gently, stirring frequently, until the chocolate has melted and is smooth. Remove from the heat and leave for about 10 minutes or until the chocolate begins to thicken slightly.

2 Cut the fruit loaf into medium to thick slices, then spread with the melted chocolate. Leave until almost set, then cut each slice in half to form a triangle. Layer the chocolate-coated bread slices and the chopped apricots in the buttered ovenproof dish.

3 Stir the cream and the milk together, then stir in the caster sugar. Beat the eggs, then gradually beat in the cream and milk mixture. Beat thoroughly until well blended. Carefully pour over the bread slices and apricots and leave to stand for 30 minutes.

4 Sprinkle with the demerara sugar and place in a roasting tin half filled with boiling water. Cook in the preheated oven for 45 minutes, or until golden and the custard is lightly set. Serve immediately.

HELPFUL HINT

It is important to leave the pudding to stand for at least 30 minutes, as described in step 3. This allows the custard to soak into the bread – otherwise it sets around the bread as it cooks, making the pudding seem stodgy.

2

3

4

Chocolate Profiteroles

INGREDIENTS

Serves 4

For the pastry:

150 ml/¼ pint water
50 g/2 oz butter
65 g/2½ oz plain flour, sifted
2 medium eggs, lightly beaten

For the custard:

300 ml/½ pint milk
pinch of freshly grated nutmeg
3 medium egg yolks
50 g/2 oz caster sugar
2 tbsp plain flour, sifted
2 tbsp cornflour, sifted

For the sauce:

175 g/6 oz soft brown sugar
150 ml/¼ pint boiling water
1 tsp instant coffee
1 tbsp cocoa powder
1 tbsp brandy
75 g/3 oz butter
1 tbsp golden syrup

1 Preheat the oven to 220°C/425°F/Gas Mark 7, 15 minutes before cooking. Lightly oil 2 baking sheets. For the pastry, place the water and the butter in a heavy-based saucepan and bring to the boil. Remove from the heat and beat in the flour. Return to the heat and cook for 1 minute or until the mixture forms a ball in the centre of the saucepan.

2 Remove from the heat and leave to cool slightly, then gradually beat in the eggs a little at a time, beating well after each addition. Once all the eggs have been added, beat until the paste is smooth and glossy. Pipe or spoon 20 small balls onto the baking sheets, allowing plenty of room for expansion.

3 Bake in the preheated oven for 25 minutes or until well risen and golden brown. Reduce the oven temperature to 180°C/350°F/Gas Mark 4. Make a hole in each ball and continue to bake for a further 5 minutes. Remove from the oven and leave to cool.

4 For the custard, place the milk and nutmeg in a heavy-based saucepan and bring to the boil. In another saucepan, whisk together the egg yolks, sugar and the flours, then beat in the hot milk. Bring to the boil and simmer, whisking constantly for 2 minutes. Cover and leave to cool.

5 Spoon the custard into the profiteroles and arrange on a large serving dish. Place all the sauce ingredients in a small saucepan and bring to the boil, then simmer for 10 minutes. Remove from the heat and cool slightly before serving with the chocolate profiteroles.

1

2

5